The Congress

GARY LEE MALECHA AND
DANIEL J. REAGAN

Student Guides to American Government and Politics
Brian Lloyd Fife, Series Editor

 GREENWOOD
™

An Imprint of ABC-CLIO, LLC
Santa Barbara, California • Denver, Colorado

Library of Congress Cataloging-in-Publication Data

Names: Malecha, Gary Lee, 1955- author. | Reagan, Daniel J. author.
Title: The Congress / Gary Lee Malecha and Daniel J. Reagan
Description: Santa Barbara, California : Greenwood, an Imprint of ABC-CLIO, 2021. |
    Series: Student guides to American government and politics | Includes bibliographical
    references and index.
Identifiers: LCCN 2021008335 (print) | LCCN 2021008336 (ebook) | ISBN
    9781440873744 (hardcover) | ISBN 9781440873751 (ebook)
Subjects: LCSH: United States. Congress. | Legislative power—United
    States.
Classification: LCC JK1021 .M36 2021 (print) | LCC JK1021 (ebook) | DDC
    328.73—dc23
LC record available at https://lccn.loc.gov/2021008335
LC ebook record available at https://lccn.loc.gov/2021008336

ISBN: 978-1-4408-7374-4 (print)
       978-1-4408-7375-1 (ebook)

25 24 23 22 21   1 2 3 4 5

This book is also available as an eBook.

Greenwood
An Imprint of ABC-CLIO, LLC

ABC-CLIO, LLC
147 Castilian Drive
Santa Barbara, California 93117
www.abc-clio.com

This book is printed on acid-free paper ∞

Manufactured in the United States of America

To our teachers and our students; to our families,
whom we love; and to the memory of our parents:
Rosemary Louise Malecha and
Joseph Valentine Malecha
and
Catherine Marie Reagan and James Thomas Reagan

Contents

Preface

The delegates who gathered at the Philadelphia constitutional convention in the summer of 1787 agreed that the legislative branch was central to the new government they were creating. They had, after all, declared independence and fought a revolutionary war against Great Britain to gain a government in which the nation's people would be represented. In their view, the success of representative, or republican, government depended on a strong legislature with the powers to create laws and craft public policy. The constitution that the delegates drafted reflected those beliefs. It created a legislative branch, in the form of the Congress, that was dependent upon the people but also equipped with a range of important powers. These included, to name just a few, the power to impose taxes, appropriate money, declare war, maintain an army and a navy, regulate commerce, establish courts, and confirm executive branch and court appointments.

Even as they assigned Congress significant authority, however, the delegates recognized that this legislative assembly needed to be subject to restraints as well. To that end, they also included important provisions that enabled the other branches of government—the executive and the judicial—to check or limit actions that each could take. The delegates also gave the people themselves the power to control the national legislative assembly through elections.

One of Congress's distinctive characteristics in the constitutional system of which it's a part is that it is the only branch elected directly by the American people. Presidents are selected by the Electoral College and not by direct, popular vote. Federal justices are not even indirectly elected but are nominated and appointed by the president and the Senate. Still, even though Congress is the first branch of government and the only branch that the people have a direct hand in choosing, many people do not fully understand or appreciate what the institution does, how it works, and the role it is supposed to play in the nation's life. Recent polls show that fewer than half of the nation's citizens know the powers of Congress or the number of senators a state has or what parties control the institution. Many cannot name their own representatives, and only a fraction of the voting age population knows the names of the institution's leaders, let alone the roles they play. Most people also have trouble recounting how legislation is enacted. And in an era when the presidency tends to dominate the U.S. political landscape, it is easy to forget the array of powers that the Constitution gives to the Congress—again, the power to declare war, to raise and maintain the armed forces, and to initiate and monitor most of the government's spending—are serious powers. Moreover, very few people approve of Congress's performance or even have confidence in it. As Republican senator Tom Coburn of Oklahoma bluntly told his former colleagues when he testified in a committee hearing in 2016, shortly after he retired from office, "America doesn't trust you anymore. That's the truth."

Congress is a perplexing and complicated body that can be hard to understand. It is divided into two chambers, with each one representing different constituencies. The House represents people, and the Senate represents states. Each chamber has a distinctive set of values and rules, and each encourages different types of behavior in its members. There are even some important differences in their constitutional responsibilities. The chambers also have different terms of office. House members, known as representatives, are elected for two years, senators for six. Congress includes many people—100 in the Senate, 435 in the House—from diverse parts of the nation, and its members represent and are responsive to a wide range of people and interests.

Congress is often overshadowed by the office of the presidency. There is only one president, who can command the attention of news media and the American people in a way that no member of Congress can. In addition, no single lawmaker or even group of lawmakers can possibly speak or act on behalf of such a diverse congressional membership.

But a failure to understand Congress can have some unfortunate political consequences. Misunderstanding Congress and the larger constitutional system of which it is a part can lead some citizens to disengage from politics altogether, others to have unrealistic expectations about what the American government can do, and still others to a kind of cynicism that threatens the fundamental public trust that is the bedrock on which healthy representative government rests.

Our goal in this book is to help you get past barriers to understanding Congress. In our introduction, we sketch a way for you to think about Congress in broad terms. Our first two chapters tell the story of how Congress was created and how it has developed over time. In the next several chapters, we focus on the different parts that make up congressional politics. We trace how those parts have changed to keep pace with the dynamic social and economic forces that transformed the country from an agrarian-based nation at the margins of world affairs to an industrial and then postindustrial country with a leading role in international politics. Along the way, we discuss the different ways that representatives and senators have been elected and describe how their behaviors, work, and responsibilities have evolved. We describe the types of committees they sit on and the parties to which they belong, and we discuss the roles both play in congressional work, as the roles have changed over time. We also touch on how members enlist the staff support and media capabilities they have at their disposal and how they have adapted their use of these to meet the different challenges they have faced. And we show how all this impacts the way that Congress carries out its work and shapes its relations with the executive and the judicial branches. After taking you through this journey, we conclude with some observations and thoughts about Congress's future as it heads deeper into its third century of existence.

Introduction: Thinking about Congress

Many people find the U.S. Congress to be one of the most frustrating features of contemporary political life. Americans who disagree with their neighbors on many issues find common ground when it comes to the Congress. Citizens from all walks of life, and with widely divergent political views, agree that their national legislature fails, often miserably, to live up to its role. These complaints come from conservatives and liberals, Republicans as well as Democrats. They come from scholars and journalists. They are voiced by people of all walks of life and from all parts of the country, ranging from the heartland to the coasts. Even former and current members of Congress contribute to this chorus of complaint. At a time when many worry that the country has become too politically divided, dissatisfaction with Congress appears to be one of the few things that binds Americans. Today, it seems that "everybody hates Congress." Yet that has almost always been the case. As one political scientist put it, "hating on Congress" is "an American tradition."[1]

CONGRESS: A CURIOUS INSTITUTION

Americans have long accused Congress of being slow and inefficient, of being dominated by self-centered people who respond more to the demands of special interests that can help them get reelected than to the nation's needs. In the late 1800s and early 1900s, Mark Twain, a writer and humorist of the time, could count on getting laughs by poking fun at Congress. He compared representatives and senators to fleas, criminals, cowards, drunks, and even to Judas Iscariot, questioning not only their integrity but their intelligence. "Suppose you were an idiot," he wrote in his autobiography. "And suppose you were a member of Congress. But I repeat myself."[2] Yet Twain's barbs about Congress were nothing new for

American political discourse. They echoed concerns raised about the nation's lawmakers almost right from the start. Fisher Ames, who served in the first four Congresses, despaired of the low arts required to make it into the nation's legislature. "To be a favorite of an ignorant multitude," he wrote, "a man must descend to their level; he must desire what they desire, and detest all that they do not approve; he must yield to their prejudices, and substitute them for principles. Instead of enlightening their errors, he must adopt them; he must furnish the sophistry that will propagate and defend them."[3]

Popular books written at different points in the last half century reflect the durability of dissatisfaction with Congress. In the 1960s, for example, Senator Joseph Clark lamented the institution's failings in a book he titled *Congress: The Sapless Branch.* More recently, two respected political scientists and longtime students of Congress offered a searing assessment of the institution's performance in *The Broken Branch: How Congress Is Failing America and How to Get It Back on Track.* Public opinion polls regularly confirm that most Americans share these sentiments. Survey data show that Congress routinely falls below the presidency and the Supreme Court in terms of the confidence that citizens have in the three branches of government.

In recent years, Congress's approval ratings have in some polls occasionally dropped to single digits. How low can congressional popularity go? As polls suggest, very low. Some polls report that Congress, at times, has been less popular than the Internal Revenue Service, lawyers, banks, traffic jams, and President Nixon during his impeachment investigation. Public approval ratings of Congress have not topped 30 percent over the last decade and recently set a record low.[4] John McCain, a Vietnam War hero who later became a member of Congress, U.S. senator, and the 2008 Republican candidate for president, often pointed to the small percentage of Americans who reported that they had a lot of confidence in the Congress and quipped, "You get down that low, you get down to blood relatives and paid staffers."

Yet here is a curious thing: although the institution is held in low esteem, members of Congress win reelection at astonishingly high rates. In the first ten congressional elections held this century (2000–2018), an average of almost 94 percent of House members who ran for reelection were returned to office. This is not a recent trend either. Over the last fifty years, from 1968 through 2018, an average of 93 percent of all House incumbents who stood for reelection won. In twelve of those twenty-six elections, the reelection rates of sitting members were over 95 percent.

While the reelection rate of incumbent senators is not as high, they also enjoy a good chance of winning at the ballot box. An average of 86 percent of senators seeking reelection in the years 2000–2018 defeated their challengers, and in the last half century, more than a majority of those running for reelection have been returned to Congress.[5] If Congress is seen to be such a rotten, dysfunctional institution, why do so many Americans keep deciding to send the same people back to Capitol Hill?

It turns out that there are other curious things about Congress. While it is true, for instance, that Congress as an institution frequently disappoints a great many people, it is also true that it has played a role in shaping many policies that have met some of the country's most daunting and vexing challenges. Those challenges include fending off European powers in the years after America first gained independence from Great Britain, promoting westward expansion in the early to mid-1800s, and seeing the nation through the Civil War and Reconstruction in the 1860s and early 1870s. Congress also responded to the seismic transformations in the American economy during the age of industrialization, which ran from the post–Civil War era through the early 1900s, and it worked to come to grips with the dramatic social and demographic changes that accompanied that very same economic revolution. Likewise, Congress had a hand in shaping the country's responses to two world wars, a worldwide depression, and the country's rise to international prominence in an age of nuclear weapons. It has grappled with the nation's long struggle for racial justice and its aspiration to treat all citizens equally. And in fits and starts, Congress has played a role in moving the nation to an advanced digital economy in the current era of globalization, open markets, and free trade.

As most of these events unfolded, Americans argued about whether Congress acted wisely or foolishly, justly or unjustly, and those conversations continue today. Yet while they regularly disagree with their neighbors about what they hope Congress will do, Americans often agree that the institution's shortcomings are mainly due to deficiencies in the character and abilities of its members. According to this common complaint, too many representatives and senators lack the ability to see and the courage to pursue the country's national interest.

While the impact that the personal characteristics of legislators have on the Congress should not be discounted, we also need to consider the extent to which Congress's performance is affected by many matters that it does not entirely control. It is, after all, an institution that is shaped as much by the Constitution, history, and the larger political landscape of which it is a part, as it is by the members who compose it.

CONSTITUTIONAL ARCHITECTURE

Many features that affect congressional behavior and performance are rooted in its constitutional architecture or design. The Constitution's framers agreed that Congress should be the first branch of government. Its representation of citizens' views, they believed, provided the key ingredient of republican, or representative, government. Still, though they wanted it to reflect citizens' views and act on their behalf, the framers also considered it prudent to create a two-chamber, or bicameral, legislative assembly. They also designed these two chambers, the House and the Senate, with important differences that have significant implications. They affect representation in Congress, yield certain behavioral responses, and impact the pace and outcomes of congressional operations.

The Constitution requires that all members of the House of Representatives stand for reelection every two years, while Senate elections are staggered so that only one-third of the senators are elected every two years. As such, each session of Congress has lawmakers chosen in three different elections or moments in political history. The shorter two-year term of representatives encourages them to focus on an election that is just over the horizon. It thus fastens that chamber's attention on prevailing public opinion or popular sentiment. In contrast, senators' longer six-year term provides them with greater freedom from prevailing public opinion. Since two-thirds of them do not need to focus on an impending election, senators are provided more latitude in their deliberations, debate, and legislative work. Furthermore, having only one-third of the Senate elected every two years provides the institution with some stability and continuity. As a result of these institutional differences, members of the two chambers often behave and see things differently.

Another constitutionally mandated design difference is that each of the fifty states, no matter how large or small its population, is guaranteed two—and only two—senators. By contrast, the number of representatives each state receives is based on the size of its population, as recorded in the national census, which is essentially a head count of all the American people that is conducted every ten years. According to the Constitution, though, each state must have at least one representative. In 1929, Congress capped the size of the House of Representatives at 435 members. Thus, every ten years after the census is completed, House seats must be redistributed to reflect population changes across the country. In the reallocation following the census, states that see large population increases gain seats and influence in the House of Representatives, while other states lose seats and influence. With the exception of those who come from states that are too small to have more than one member, each House member represents roughly 750,000 people.

This realignment of representation, however, is limited to the House. Since the Constitution requires each state to have two—and only two—senators, changing population patterns do not translate into changing levels of representation or influence in the Senate. This has important implications for the representative nature of Congress. Population has no impact whatsoever on a state's influence in the Senate. So, for instance, the twenty least populous states, home to only about 10 percent of the American population, are given 40 percent of the Senate's one hundred seats. Here is another way to understand the magnitude of the Senate's disconnect between population and representation. Every state is divided into a number of smaller political subdivisions called counties. There are a number of counties located all over the United States with larger populations than some states, but the states with smaller populations have just as much say in Senate matters as the states with those counties do.[6] Los Angeles County alone, home to the city of Los Angeles, has a population of over ten million people. If it were a state, this one county would be the tenth-largest state in the Union.[7] The structure of the Senate achieves the framers' objective of giving states, as well as citizens, a say in congressional activity. But it also gives a smaller number of people more influence than they would have if Congress represented only people and not states.[8]

Another outcome of the Congress's constitutional design concerns lawmakers' constituencies. Since most House members represent a smaller number of citizens from smaller geographic areas than do senators, it is often the case that they represent a more homogenous constituency than their Senate counterparts. With but a few exceptions, most senators represent a more diverse citizenry. At times, this encourages them to work for legislative outcomes that have broader appeal than those sought by House members, who represent a narrower set of citizen interests within a district rather than a state. To be sure, this is not always the case; seven states have so few people that they only have one House seat, and in those instances the representatives' constituencies are the same as their colleagues in the Senate—the citizens of the entire state. Yet a majority of senators, most of the time, represent a more varied group of citizens than do House members.

Despite all these unique design elements, which often give representatives and senators a different perspective on issues before them, the Constitution requires that in order to pass a law, both chambers must pass a bill that is identical to the one passed by the other body in every single respect. Regardless of whether they represent different types of constituencies or are closer to or more removed from direct electoral pressure, members in both chambers must agree on the exact language if they want to pass a law. In some time periods, this constitutionally mandated bar has been easier for Congress to reach than in other times, but it is often a real obstacle to legislators. While many Americans throughout time have blamed members for the slow pace that often marks congressional policy making—citing self-centeredness, indifference, or even laziness—they often overlook the institutional design features that usually make it difficult for Congress to act with the speed and decisiveness American citizens desire.

CONGRESSIONAL RELATIONS AND HISTORICAL CHANGE

The Constitution prescribes Congress's relationship with the other branches of government. While it gives most legislative powers to the Congress, it also gives the president a meaningful role in the legislative process. This interdependence ensures that Congress will have a more continuous—and often more contentious—relationship with the presidency than it does with the judicial branch.

To become law, a bill passed by the House and Senate must be signed by the president. If the president disagrees with a bill sent by Congress, the president can veto, or reject, it. Unless Congress can muster a supermajority, or two-thirds, vote of both the House and the Senate to override that veto, the bill dies. In addition, in most cases the president is obliged to spend money to achieve the policy goals reflected in laws that Congress passes. However, a president has the power to impound or not spend that money, thus delaying the law's implementation.

Similarly, while the president is the head of the executive branch, the Constitution gives Congress some important inroads into executive affairs. The heads of executive departments, as well as other important executive offices, need to receive Senate approval before assuming those positions, and most of the money that the executive branch relies on is determined by the House and Senate. Representatives and senators also have the obligation and the power to oversee executive branch activity to be sure that laws are being faithfully executed. And while the Constitution gives the president the power to nominate individuals to serve as federal judges and to make treaties with other countries, it also gives the Senate the power to reject those nominees and negotiated treaties.

Relations between Congress and the president are also complicated by the fact that Article II of the Constitution gives the president a constituency and electoral timetable different from that of the House and the Senate. Presidents compete for votes in a national election, whereas members of Congress are elected in what might be thought of as regional competitions. And the length of the president's four-year term is halfway between that of a representative and a senator. Just as differences in constituencies and elections affect the working relationship between the House and Senate, they also shape and partially explain relations between Congress and the presidency. In both instances, these differences make cooperation more difficult.

Unlike many other democracies, the American system is not a parliamentary one. A parliamentary system is structured to give control of both the legislative and executive capacities of the government to one party. A parliamentary government's prime minister—the nation's chief executive officer and the president's counterpart, so to speak—is also a member of the legislature. So the majority parties in these sorts of democracies, or the coalition of parties that together constitute a legislative majority, have all of the votes they need to pass their policy proposals. Parliamentary majorities usually have no need to compromise with legislators in the minority. Moreover, there is no independent executive that can veto their bills or implement them in a way that frustrates the goals of the parliamentary majority. The United States' Constitution explicitly prohibits this sort of arrangement. It forbids any one individual from serving simultaneously in more than one branch of government, so in that sense the American legislature and executive are physically separated from each other. The bicameral Congress, especially when each chamber is controlled by a different party, further complicates the American legislative process. Passing a law in the United States regularly requires lawmakers to negotiate with policy makers in different chambers and branches, all of whom operate under different electoral timetables and may belong to different parties. These structural features, having nothing to do with the character or ability of representatives and senators, are another reason that the Congress often moves more slowly than some hope.

The constitutional linking of the legislative and executive branches affects congressional behavior in still other ways, drawing attention to even more forces to consider in thinking about Congress. Since these two branches are so intertwined in much of their work, each one has an incentive to adjust its behavior in response to the other, as even a brief history of the relationship between the two shows.

One of the things that has had a great influence on presidential behavior, organization, and power is the country's role in international politics. After World War II, the United States emerged as a global leader and assumed a leadership role among Western democracies. To meet these new responsibilities, subsequent presidents sought and largely gained a broad range of new powers and resources. The number of assistants and staff members able to advance presidential goals in this post–World War II world grew significantly with the creation of new executive agencies. By the 1950s, the country had also decided for the first time in its history that it needed to maintain a large, permanent, professional, peacetime military force to defend American interests across the globe.

At roughly the same time, the role of the presidency increased its leverage in domestic affairs. Elected in 1932 shortly after the start of the Great Depression in 1929, President Franklin D. Roosevelt assumed responsibility for managing the nation's prosperity. His New Deal programs brought with them new authority and resources. This contributed to a growth in presidential staff and support agencies. It also increased governmental expenditures over which presidents could exert their control. The president's expanding imprint on domestic affairs continued through the 1950s and on into the 1960s and 1970s as the country addressed other national problems. These included civil rights, poverty, a slowing economy, and a growing demand for increased social services and more environmental protections.

Congress responded to these changes in the executive branch that were brought about by an expanding policy agenda. It reorganized its committee system to align with its changing workload. It also created a host of legislative agencies designed to give Congress the technical and policy expertise it needed to compete with the president's array of new agencies, assistants, and powers. Congress created a new budgeting procedure with the hope of making more rational budgetary decisions. It created agencies to improve its research and budgetary capabilities and its understanding of technology. Congress also expanded the number of staff personnel that representatives and senators could hire, and both chambers expanded the number of staff members assigned to their committees. As the 1970s ended, the professional and policy expertise that Congress could draw on was more robust and much more impressive than what had been available to it in the past.

Yet by the late 1970s, other forces were at work that would induce another round of change in presidential behavior, which in turn encouraged even more congressional reforms. One of those changes was rooted in the civil rights struggles that took center stage in American politics in the 1960s. Between the 1930s and the 1960s, both the Republicans and the Democrats were internally divided. Each party had a liberal and a conservative wing. As such, the leaders of the two parties had an incentive to suppress issues that threatened to split the sometimes-fragile alliance that kept each of them together. Civil rights was one such issue. Liberal northern and midwestern Democrats and Republicans were more interested in pushing a civil rights agenda than were the more conservative southern Democrats and some western Republicans. After Democratic president John F. Kennedy's assassination in 1963, his vice president, Lyndon Johnson, a fellow Democrat who had represented Texas in both the House and Senate, became president and decided to push a more aggressive civil rights agenda. Johnson's success brought about new alignments within the parties. By the late 1980s, the parties had changed. They became more ideologically unified, or cohesive, as liberals gravitated to the Democratic

Party and conservatives moved into the ranks of their Republican opponents.

In 1980, the country elected Republican Ronald W. Reagan as president. To advance his agenda, Reagan pursued a novel communications strategy. Instead of spending as much time as earlier presidents had bargaining with members of Congress to reach policy agreements, Reagan used television to make direct appeals to the American people. Looking into the camera in a series of nationally televised broadcasts, he urged citizens to contact their congressional representatives and encourage them to enact his conservative policy agenda. He was so effective with this strategy that he won the nickname "the Great Communicator," and at least on some issues for a short period of time, he was able to get even the Democratic-controlled House to pass his legislative initiatives. Determined to defend themselves against Reagan's communications juggernaut, Democrats encouraged their leaders to mount a counteroffensive. Democratic leaders responded by expanding and using their media resources to challenge the president and to attack his initiatives.

Similar changes in party outreach to the general public were afoot with House Republicans. Representative Newt Gingrich, a Republican from Georgia elected in 1978, understood that new communication technologies and strategies could be applied to gain power and transform congressional operations. He created an organization, called GOPAC, that trained potential Republican candidates on how to talk effectively on television—for instance, to only speak in short sentences so that station editors wouldn't have to edit comments to fit the short time they could devote to any one story. GOPAC also distributed money and other resources that Republican candidates needed to run effective campaigns. Gingrich argued that Republicans should stop compromising with their Democratic opponents. He believed that one of the reasons Republicans had not been the majority party in the House since the late 1950s was that voters didn't see enough difference between the two parties. Instead of trying to find common ground with Democrats, Gingrich taught his followers to use their newly acquired communications skills to talk directly to voters and accentuate how Republicans differed from Democrats. Among the topics he urged his followers to emphasize were reducing social welfare benefits, returning power to the states, lowering taxes, and relying more on market forces than on government regulations. When the Gingrich-led Republicans became the majority House party in the 1994 midterm election for the first time in forty years and Gingrich took over as House Speaker, his more partisan and divisive style of political communication was widely adopted by both parties and eventually in both chambers.

Changes in media technology continued to influence both presidential and congressional practices and behaviors. In the 1960s and 1970s, most

Americans got their political news from a small array of media outlets—the three major network television stations and a handful of nationally read newspapers. In the 1980s, cable television started to expand the places where citizens could get political news, and that expansion really took off in the 1990s. In 1987, the Federal Communications Commission eliminated what is known as the Fairness Doctrine, which required news venues to give equal coverage to both sides of a political issue. Doing away with the Fairness Doctrine meant that radio stations that ran political talk shows no longer had to provide "balanced" coverage. Political conservatives swiftly responded to take advantage of this new ruling. They created many new "talk-radio" programs that allowed them to amplify their political goals and values and gain the trust of listeners who shared their partisan perspective. The Internet also emerged in the 1990s, and it quickly evolved into yet another platform to deliver political news and campaign messages. Social media like Facebook, YouTube, Instagram, Snapchat, and others soon followed. In this changing media environment, news providers soon found that to survive they needed to attract smaller, but intensely loyal and usually more partisan, "niche" audiences. Just as the parties were becoming ideologically separate and partisan, so, too, were many news media sources. These dual trends, which continually fed off one another, further changed how Congress carried out its work and how citizens perceived and responded to its activities.

As a result of all these factors, today's Congress is composed of—and organized by—parties that strongly oppose one another. Members rarely reach across the aisle these days, and they frequently attack and dismiss their partisan opponents and their policies when they appear in public forums and news outlets. Indeed, it is these sorts of contentious features of congressional politics that many Americans point to when they explain why they have such little faith in their national legislature. Yet the roots of many of these problems, which are a product of Congress's design and history, and of changes on the larger political landscape, are frequently overlooked when people think about and evaluate Congress as an institution.

Still, while hardly revered, Congress has endured. It has managed to weather change and considerable criticism for more than two centuries, and it has contributed greatly, if not always wisely and decisively, to the development of the United States. Congress continues to play a key role in American political life. The chapters that follow will show how the institution has adapted to change and developed the structures and operations that, however flawed they may be, have enabled the U.S. Congress to become the most powerful legislative assembly in the world. After exploring Congress's early beginnings and growth, the book then examines its membership, organization, structure, and operations as well as its relations with the other branches of government and other political actors and groups. The book concludes with some observations about challenges facing Congress as it moves into the future.

NOTES

1. Keith E. Whittington, "Hating on Congress: An American Tradition," *Gallup Blog*, June 30, 2019, https://news.gallup.com/opinion/gallup/262316/hating-congress-american-tradition.aspx.

2. "Congress," Mark Twain Quotations, accessed June 27, 2020, http://www.twainquotes.com/Congress.html.

3. Fisher Ames, "American Literature (1803)," *American Political Thought*, by Keith E. Whittington, accessed June 27, 2020, https://global.oup.com/us/companion.websites/fdscontent/uscompanion/us/static/companion.websites/9780199338863/whittington_updata/ch_4_ames_american_literature.pdf.

4. Ezra Klein, "Congressional Dysfunction," Vox, May 15, 2015, https://www.vox.com/2015/1/2/18089154/congressional-dysfunction; and Harry Enten, "Congress's Approval Rating Hasn't Hit 30% in 10 Years. That's a Record," CNN, June 1, 2019, https://www.cnn.com/2019/06/01/politics/poll-of-the-week-congress-approval-rating/index.html.

5. "Reelection Rates over the Years," OpenSecrets, accessed June 27, 2020, https://www.opensecrets.org/overview/reelect.php.

6. See, for instance, https://external-preview.redd.it/W30cfzbixSUZ8poTD5wkxzWFCpFMFLZcl0R85soAybM.png?auto=webp&s=25dfaa0de954c5ea5c6c6d8230f0f8fc584cc3a1.

7. Here is a visual presentation that compares the population of Los Angeles County to the population of other states: http://www.laalmanac.com/population/po04a.php.

8. Sergio Peçanha, "Are Cows Better Represented in the Senate Than People?" *Washington Post*, January 16, 2020, https://www.washingtonpost.com/opinions/2020/01/16/are-cows-better-represented-senate-than-people.

1

Creating the Congress

Delegates attending the constitutional convention in Philadelphia during the summer of 1787 agreed the government established by the Articles of Confederation, their country's first constitution, was not up to the task of providing the security and stability the new nation required. The constitution that they struggled to put together over the course of nearly three months that summer was, they believed, a practical solution that promised to address their current government's weaknesses while preserving citizens' liberties and rights. The document they ultimately produced was the result of a combination of ideas, negotiations, political maneuvering, and a series of concessions and compromises.[1]

WEAKNESSES OF THE ARTICLES OF CONFEDERATION

Written during the Revolutionary War and finally ratified by all states in 1781, the Articles of Confederation provided for a fragile alliance between the states, which were reluctant to give up control of their own affairs. The government it created was structurally simple, had limited authority, and was hard to change. It consisted of a unicameral (single chamber) Congress or legislative assembly that represented the thirteen different states as sovereign, equal entities. Each state was allotted one vote, regardless of its land area or population.

Lacking important powers, the government faltered almost from the start. It could not regulate interstate commerce. It struggled to raise revenue and maintain order. Despite its glaring weaknesses, however, this constitution that defined the government's powers could not be easily changed. Amendments needed unanimous approval. This made it next to impossible for Congress to get the additional authority it sorely needed. Conflicts between states centering on trade and currency were commonplace and not easily resolved. States frequently refused to comply with the Congress's decisions and often expanded their own powers at its expense. As frustrations grew, support for a new constitutional framework for the young nation increased.

THE EARLY DAYS OF THE CONVENTION AND JAMES MADISON'S PLAN

The convention's fifty-five delegates, which included representatives from all states except Rhode Island, brought to the proceedings a wealth of knowledge that informed their deliberations. As they addressed the Articles' problems, they drew on insights derived from their lives as British citizens and revolutionaries, their study of political theory and the history of government and the law, and their direct involvement in political activities. Many had served in colonial assemblies prior to the revolution as well as in state legislatures afterward. Roughly three-fourths of them had, at one time or another, even represented their states in the national legislature created by the Articles of Confederation. They also shared the belief, common in the postrevolutionary era, that "legislatures—composed of representatives answerable to the people—were the heart and soul of any system of truly 'republican' government."[2] For them, as their own experience and study confirmed, a sufficiently empowered legislative body that was representative of the people and carefully designed and subject to restraints was key to having a government that protected individual liberties.

James Madison had pondered the Articles' failings for quite some time. Having served in the national Congress under the Articles as well as in the Virginia state legislature, he witnessed many of its shortcomings at both the state and national levels of government. Even before he made the trip to Philadelphia, he had concluded that small adjustments to the Articles would not be enough to provide the sort of government such a new and expansive nation required. Believing wholesale change was in order, Madison used the days leading up to the opening of the constitutional convention's proceedings to confer with other Virginia delegates to sketch out a plan for a more powerful central government. His goal was to have something ready for the other members to consider when they began their assembly's deliberations.

Madison's proposal for a new government called for a stronger, more responsible legislative body. It also incorporated separation of powers, adding an executive branch and a judiciary. Edmund Randolph, a fellow delegate from Virginia, introduced the plan during the first week of the convention. Known as the Virginia Plan, it became the focus of the members' early discussions and decisions and ultimately set the stage for dramatic constitutional change.

The Virginia Plan's reforms of the national legislature promised a bold departure from the one in place. Madison's blueprint called for replacing the Articles' unicameral Congress with a two-chamber, or bicameral, legislative assembly. This move to adopt a bicameral legislature did not faze most delegates. After all, they had a long history with bicameral legislatures. These included the British Parliament as well as many of their own colonial assemblies. In addition, almost all the states represented at the convention established bicameral legislatures when they rewrote their constitutions during the revolutionary era. Delegates were also well versed in arguments in favor of bicameral legislatures. They well knew, as they often reminded one another, that legislatures could not always be trusted to behave responsibly. As experienced and practical politicians, they thus recognized that any legislative assembly equipped with substantial authority, while important for republican government, needed to be restrained, and they generally agreed that one of the ways of doing that was to divide it into two chambers, as the Virginia Plan proposed.[3]

The formula for allocating representatives in the Virginia Plan's bicameral legislature was considerably different from the one the Articles used to determine states' representation in the Confederation's Congress. The Virginia Plan's legislature would represent people, not states. The number of congressional seats a state would receive in each chamber would be based on the "number of free inhabitants" residing within the state or its "quotas of contribution." In practice, this meant giving states with larger populations and greater wealth more power. The plan also called for direct election of representatives who sat in the first chamber, while those in the second chamber would be indirectly selected by members of the first chamber, who would select from candidates supplied to them by the different state legislatures.

The Virginia Plan also aimed to increase the authority of the legislative branch. It proposed entrusting this new bicameral Congress with sweeping powers to act in those cases "to which the separate States are incompetent." It also called for giving it power to veto actions taken by individual state legislatures. This would ensure supremacy of the national government over the states, which Madison considered vital to the federal government's success.

OPPOSITION TO THE VIRGINIA PLAN

The Virginia Plan met stiff resistance as the convention's deliberations proceeded. Much of the opposition focused on its proposed legislative branch. Many delegates feared it would amass too much power. Some harbored reservations about giving Congress nearly open-ended authority to act in those instances in "which the separate States are incompetent." A number also raised concerns about giving it an unqualified veto over the legislative actions of individual states, for they feared it would be used to consolidate power in the central government.

In addition, delegates voiced reservations about how the Virginia Plan dealt with the challenge of selecting legislators. Some thought its selection process was too democratic. These delegates feared that directly electing members to the first branch would bring to Congress too many representatives who would be overly responsive to the momentary passions of people who were often ill informed. They anticipated that this would produce bad legislation and unstable government. A much smaller number of delegates disagreed. They felt the election process was not democratic enough. Indirect selection of members for the second branch, they believed, would make it hard for constituents to hold lawmakers accountable for what they did in office. These delegates also suggested that anything short of direct election would make it difficult for this new government to gain the people's confidence.

TURNING POINT OF THE CONVENTION

Despite these differences of opinion, ingredients for a compromise gradually revealed themselves. Most delegates agreed that direct election for one chamber, which would later become the House of Representatives, would go a long way in ensuring the representation of popular interests that republican government required. They also more or less concurred that biennial elections (elections every two years) would provide terms that would be long enough for representatives to gain familiarity with national policy issues yet short enough for constituents to hold them accountable through elections.

At the same time, most at the convention believed that the other chamber, the one that would eventually be called the Senate, should consist of members capable of correcting the House's potential weaknesses. It needed, as Madison told the convention, to be able to proceed "with more coolness, with more system, & with more wisdom, than the popular branch."[4] Delegates thus ultimately agreed that senators should have longer terms—six years—and be elected indirectly by their respective state legislatures. Longer terms meant that the Senate would have greater continuity and stability. Its members would have more time to amass knowledge necessary to carry out their legislative responsibilities and be positioned to furnish additional insights that members of the House, because of their shorter term of office, could not provide. Their longer terms also meant that senators would likely have more independence from public opinion than their House colleagues would when making decisions. Convention delegates also generally agreed that indirect election of senators by state legislators, many of whom would be more knowledgeable about politics and policy issues than ordinary voters, would furnish the Senate with individuals who were less inclined to bend to their constituents' momentary passions or whims.

These decisions on the selection process, however, left unaddressed two significant fault lines that divided the convention. Both centered on who lawmakers would represent. The first clash involved whether slaves would be included in calculating the number of representatives allocated to states. Delegates from southern states wanted to count slaves in apportioning the number of a state's representatives. Most southerners viewed slaves as property and a source of wealth, and they believed that wealth should be included in any formula that determined representation. Many from the North disagreed, though their opposition was primarily rooted in self-interest as well. They felt that this special treatment the South was asking for was unfair and would put their own states at a disadvantage. Few of them stopped to confront directly the fundamental immorality of slavery. In fact, most felt that they needed to accommodate the South in some way if they were to succeed in getting a new government off the ground. Southern states eventually prevailed—but only to a degree. Delegates agreed to compromise and count every slave as three-fifths of a person in determining the number of representatives to allot to each state. As a result, southern slave states would hold an advantage over the North in political representation until after the Civil War, when slavery was abolished by the ratification of the Thirteenth Amendment to the Constitution.

The other fault line concerned the allocation of political power among states with dramatically different levels of population and land. Delegates from the less populous states feared their interests would be constantly overridden by large states if, as the Virginia Plan proposed, states with bigger populations received greater congressional representation. They wanted to maintain the Articles' equal representation of states and the security it provided.

Delegates from the smaller states so strongly opposed the Virginia Plan's abandonment of equal representation of states that they decided to offer an alternative proposal. Introduced by William Paterson, of New Jersey, delegates frequently referred to it as the New Jersey Plan. It called for amending the Articles to give the legislative branch the authority to raise revenue and regulate interstate commerce. It also included provisions to add an executive branch and a judiciary. Finally, it proposed changing the Articles to stipulate that laws and treaties enacted by the national government would be the supreme law of the land, something that would be later incorporated in the Constitution as Article VI's "supremacy clause."

Many of the New Jersey Plan's provisions were not far removed from those offered by the Virginia delegation. Still, there were important differences between the two plans. These centered on the legislative branch and representation. The New Jersey Plan kept intact a unicameral Congress, and it retained equal representation of states, regardless of the size of their populations.

The biggest stumbling block in the minds of most of the delegates was not the number of chambers, since only delegates from the state of Pennsylvania raised even the faintest concern about bicameralism when it was introduced in the Virginia Plan. The real problem, instead, was about power.[5] This issue directly pitted delegates from the less populous states against those from larger ones, and it provoked heated and lengthy discussions. Neither of the two blocs seemed willing to budge. As the debate on representation wore on, some delegates worried the entire convention might be derailed. To avoid failure, delegates agreed to appoint a committee with the charge of finding a solution that could end this stalemate.

The "grand committee," as it came to be known, included a member from every state at the convention. Its members drew on several ideas previously advanced during the proceedings as it drafted a proposal to resolve the convention's stalemate. The committee's solution came in the form of a bargain known as the Great Compromise. Championed by Connecticut delegates Roger Sherman and Oliver Ellsworth, it is also commonly referred to as the Connecticut Compromise. This historic agreement gave something to both sides. It provided for representation in the first branch of Congress, the House of Representatives, to be apportioned by population. Under this provision, more populous states would send more lawmakers to the House than low-population states would. It also held that all bills raising revenue or tax legislation would start with the House, a body where the more populous states would hold greater sway. This represented a partial win for the larger states. Small states received something as well. The compromise provided for the equal representation of states in the other chamber, the Senate. Somewhat later in the proceedings, delegates agreed to give each state two senators. This meant that less populous states would have just as much representation in that body as states with ten or even a hundred times their population.

Not everybody was happy with the deal. Some, like Madison, continued to push for proportional representation in the Senate as well as in the House of Representatives. Yet sentiment within the convention shifted in the direction of accepting the compromise and going forward. While other difficult choices on the design and workings of the new government still needed to be made, the Great Compromise made it possible for the convention to move ahead and finish its task of reporting out a new constitution.

POWERS OF CONGRESS

As they turned their attention to defining the specific powers of Congress, delegates agreed to drop the Virginia Plan's proposal to give Congress veto power over state laws. A growing number of them feared it would give Congress too much authority over states. Many also felt a legislative assembly that had a wide range of powers and represented such a diverse collection of states' interests would have neither the time nor the mastery of the information necessary to exercise such a power responsibly. In place of the congressional veto over state laws, they agreed to include a modified version of the New Jersey Plan's "supremacy clause," and they gave state and national courts the responsibility of upholding it. This became part of Article VI in the final draft of the Constitution.

Delegates also decided to modify the Virginia Plan's rather open-ended grant of authority to legislate on all those matters in which states by themselves were not capable of acting. While they all sought a stronger central government, they wanted to make sure it would not abuse its powers. One way to do that was by spelling out the legislature's authority.[6] They did this by enumerating the powers of Congress in Article I, Section 8. There they explicitly assigned it, among other things, the power to tax, spend, and borrow money; the power to raise and maintain a military; the power to declare war; the power to regulate commerce between states and foreign countries; the power to coin money and regulate currencies and weights and measures; the power to establish post offices and post roads; the power to give patents; and the power to create lower-level courts below the Supreme Court.

Most of the members, however, recognized that they could not specify everything in advance. They anticipated that Congress would occasionally need some latitude in how it carried out its Article I responsibilities. They provided this important freedom to act by adding the "necessary and proper" clause at the end of Article I, Section 8. This provision, which drew few objections when it was inserted, entrusts Congress with the power "to make all Laws which shall be necessary and proper for carrying into Execution the foregoing Powers, and all other powers vested by this Constitution in the Government of the United States, or any Department or Officer thereof." Over the course of history, Congress would use this provision, commonly referred to as the "elastic clause," to expand the role of the central government in ways that many at the convention would never have anticipated.[7]

Members of the convention included specific references to congressional authority elsewhere in the Constitution as well. In Article III, Section 3, for instance, they gave Congress the "power to declare punishment of treason," and in Article IV, Section 3, they entrusted it with the power to admit new states into the union and to "make all needful rules and regulations respecting the territory or other property belonging to the United States." They also gave Congress a role to play in amending the Constitution. The delegates included a provision in Article V that enabled Congress, by two-thirds vote in each house, to initiate amendments or to call for a constitutional convention to propose amendments if requested by two-thirds of the states. They also left it up to Congress to determine if state legislatures or state conventions would be used to ratify proposed amendments.

LIMITATIONS ON CONGRESSIONAL POWER

Delegates also agreed to add constitutional language that imposed specific limits on the legislature. They inserted these restrictions in Article I, Section 9. There they specifically prohibited Congress from taking certain actions. They denied it the power to ban the slave trade before 1808. They limited its authority to suspend a writ of habeas corpus, which is a petition that requires a public official to bring before a judge individuals who are being detained in prison and to explain why they are being held. The framers considered this a fundamental protection of liberty, so they stipulated in Article I, Section 9, that it could only be suspended to ensure "public safety" in cases of rebellion or invasion. Delegates also agreed to put in that section language that, among other things, placed limits on Congress's power to levy taxes and duties. In addition, they prohibited the legislature from passing bills of attainder (legislation that singles out a person or group of persons as guilty of a crime without holding a trial), as well as ex post facto laws (legislation that declares an action illegal after it has been committed). Delegates did, however, affirm congressional control of the government's purse strings in Article I, Section 9. There they stipulated that funds could not be taken from the public treasury unless first appropriated by Congress.

Given their understanding of government and their experience with it, delegates were also realistic enough to know that simply specifying in writing what the different parts of the government could or could not do would not be enough to prevent a stronger central government from going beyond its specified authority. As Madison and several others repeatedly cautioned in debates with fellow delegates, they needed to structure government so that each branch—Congress, the executive, and the judiciary—would be able to prevent the others from abusing their powers. This, according to Madison, would help "guarantee the provisions on paper" they had made.[8] The way they put this "guarantee" into practice was to distribute powers between the legislature, the executive, and the judiciary in such a way that each had the chance to influence the behavior of the other two. The delegates understood that this "sharing" of powers would often lead to what some might call an inefficient policy-making process, but they believed that it increased the chances that the new government would preserve the rights and liberties of the American people.

The delegates agreed to a series of provisions to preserve the independence of the two chambers of Congress as they conducted their legislative business and worked with the judicial and executive branches of government. They left it to each of the two chambers to establish their own rules and procedures to control their activities. They also left it to each of them to determine how to punish them for behavior considered unsuitable for their chamber, or even expel them for violating a law. They specified in the Constitution that members of the House of Representatives would elect their own presiding officer, the Speaker of the House. They also included safeguards in the Constitution to protect members' "freedom of speech and debate" in the course of legislative business, stipulating that legislators would "be privileged from arrest" in civil cases while attending congressional sessions.[9] Finally, because they feared that the president might use appointment powers to influence members' decisions in legislative proceedings, the delegates agreed to prohibit members of Congress from serving as officers in the executive branch while continuing their service in the legislature.

Delegates also incorporated in their constitutional design a series of checks and balances. They included these measures to ensure that no one branch of government, including the Congress, would become too powerful. They left it to the president to enforce the laws Congress enacted. While they gave Congress the power to declare war, they made the president commander in chief of the armed forces. They imposed limits on presidential power by entrusting Congress with the power to establish executive offices and determine the conditions of appointment to those offices. They imposed a check on Congress by giving the president power to veto legislation. In turn, they gave Congress the power to override a presidential veto with two-thirds vote in each chamber. Convention delegates left it to Congress to create all courts below the Supreme Court established in Article III. They also ceded Congress the authority to establish the jurisdiction of such courts, fix the size of the Supreme Court, and determine the types of cases that could be appealed to it from lower courts. The framers charged Congress with the power to remove judges and executive branch officials, including the president, for committing "treason, bribery, or other high crimes and misdemeanors." Following the British practice, which gave the House of Commons the power to bring charges and the House of Lords the power to judge the case, they assigned the House of Representatives "the sole power of impeachment" and gave the Senate power to remove an impeached official if two-thirds of its "members present" voted in favor of a conviction.

Delegates also included provisions that gave the Senate a special role to play in filling executive branch and court vacancies and in the treaty-making process. Believing that the Senate would be a more stable body populated by more enlightened and independent political leaders, the delegates agreed to have the Senate give its "advice and consent" to appointments made by the president to the courts and the executive branch as well as to treaties negotiated by the president.

THE END OF THE CONVENTION

After more than three months of debates, political maneuvering, and bargaining in the Philadelphia assembly, delegates concluded their deliberations. By the middle of September, they finished their work on drafting a new constitution to be submitted to the Articles' Congress and the thirteen states for their consideration. Not all members were completely happy with their constitutional handiwork. Three of the forty-one members present at the end of the proceedings refused to endorse it, and several others still harbored reservations about one provision or another. A handful of them would even lead the opposition to it when it went to the states for their approval.

Most of the delegates, however, believed that they had produced a stronger central government that promised to correct the Articles' failings to meet the needs of their geographically large, diverse, and growing republic. They did so by keeping the core institution of a republic—a legislative assembly—at the center of this proposed government, and though they agreed to cede it more power than they had given the legislature under the Articles of Confederation, they took a number of precautions to keep it from abusing its authority. They ensured that it would be representative of, and accountable to, the people through elections. These elections would be held either directly, as was the case of the House of Representatives, or indirectly, as was the case of a Senate that would be chosen by the state legislatures. They diminished Congress's ability to overstep its boundaries or engage in rash behavior. They did this by dividing it in into two different chambers, enumerating its powers, and specifying actions it could not take. They also introduced safeguards to keep a kind of balance of power between Congress and the other two branches of the federal government.

Once they finalized the draft of the document, the delegates sent it forward to the sitting Congress for its consideration. After it reviewed the delegates' finished work and recommendations, the Articles' national Congress agreed to send it to the states so that they could act on it. For the new Constitution to go into effect, it had to secure the approval of nine of the thirteen different states. Each state was called upon to hold a ratifying convention for the purpose of deciding if it wanted to get rid of the Articles and adopt this new Constitution and form of government.

As states started electing delegates to these conventions, supporters of this new Constitution prepared to make their case in these conventions. Their opponents across the several states followed suit, slowly gaining their footing and joining the debate. These opponents argued that the government under the new Constitution, and especially the Congress, was incompatible with republican government. While outnumbered, these opponents were vocal and influential and included some of the nation's most respected political figures.

Some, like Patrick Henry, an early revolutionary leader and well-known Virginia politician, had been suspicious of the Philadelphia assembly's work from the start. A few others, including Elbridge Gerry, Luther Martin, and George Mason, had attended the convention and participated in its debates and deliberations but left without endorsing the Constitution it produced. Since supporters of the new Constitution frequently referred to themselves as federalists, those who opposed the Constitution were often referred to as antifederalists. They were key participants in many of the state ratification debates, and they also extended the reach of their arguments by publishing their views in pamphlets and in letters to newspapers. While we know that the federalists went on to win the ratification debate and that the country adopted the proposed Constitution, many antifederalist ideas echoed down through the ages, and their distrust of central authority and their affinity for state governments reappeared at other critical moments in American political history.

THE ANTIFEDERALIST OPPOSITION

The antifederalists feared the new Constitution concentrated too much power in the national government. They believed that individual rights were best protected in small republics, where government was closer to the people it represented and more accurately reflected their interests.[10] Not all their objections centered on the structure and workings of this proposed government's Congress, but as its first and most potentially powerful branch, the Congress attracted a great deal of their attention and criticism.

Most of their concerns centered on the powers of Congress, how representative it would be, and the role it would play in the activities of the other branches of government. Antifederalists believed that the Constitution did not adequately confine congressional authority. They felt that even though it enumerated the legislature's powers, the document contained too many dangerous loopholes. These loopholes, they asserted, would enable Congress to expand its reach into people's lives in unwelcome and unpredictable ways. They thought the "necessary and proper" clause was simply too ambiguous and warned that it could be easily manipulated by clever politicians to advance their own policy preferences at the expense of the community's interest.

Some of them also raised concerns about the "supremacy clause." To them, this provision was troubling, especially considering the broad authority granted to Congress under the "necessary and proper" clause. They were especially worried that a strong Congress, such as the one proposed in the Constitution, would undertake sweeping use of the broad authority granted to it by the "necessary and proper" clause to undertake legislative initiatives that, when combined with the "supremacy clause," would likely preempt or undercut states' authority as well as consolidate power in the central government.[11] Finally, antifederalists were concerned that the proposed Constitution did not include a bill of rights to protect citizens from the government. In their view, without some sort of declaration of rights in the Constitution, a powerful Congress would be inclined to extend its reach in ways that would undermine individual liberties.

Antifederalists also thought the proposed Congress would not be sufficiently representative of the people. From the antifederalists' perspective, even the House of Representatives, the chamber directly elected by the people, would still be too far removed from the citizenry and would not be large enough to reflect the diverse interests and groups spread across the nation. They argued that two years was too long a time between elections and that representatives would not be sufficiently responsive to what citizens wanted government to do. They also argued that the House would not have enough members to represent the wide range of constituents in their home states. Because lawmakers would have to represent so many constituents, citizens would have a hard time getting their voices heard in the House. It would also make it harder for lawmakers to understand the people's specific needs. Quite simply, they feared this proposed House would be too small to reflect adequately the diversity of interests and views it was called on to represent.

The Senate, meanwhile, posed an even greater concern for the antifederalists. They asserted that senators indirectly elected for six-year terms to represent an entire state would be even less accountable and thus less responsive to the people's interests than lawmakers in the House of Representatives. They feared the Senate would be too aristocratic and its membership too out of touch with the people it was supposed to represent. This was especially troubling to them, since the delegates at the convention had assigned the Senate unique and important roles to play. These included "a very considerable share" of the executive branch's power regarding choosing federal judges, filling important administration positions, and making treaties with other countries.[12]

Another important problem, observed the antifederalists, was the degree to which the convention delegates blended powers between the different branches of government. For example, they contended that the writers of the Constitution had gone too far in giving Congress authority in activities traditionally understood to belong to the president, such as the Senate's involvement in the treaty process. They argued that the way the framers of the Constitution blended some powers would make the government too complex and hard for citizens to understand and control. Some also believed that congressional involvement in such activities would give Congress, and especially the Senate, undue leverage over the other branches of government.

FEDERALISTS URGE RATIFICATION

Supporters of the new Constitution, the federalists, gave little ground to their opponents. They aggressively pushed their case for this proposed government. Like the antifederalists, they made their arguments in the ratifying conventions held in the different states as well as in newspapers and pamphlets. They believed and argued that a new government at least as powerful as the one proposed by the convention's delegates was necessary to secure the liberties they had fought to gain in the Revolutionary War. Of the many arguments made in support of the ratification of the Constitution, the most important and influential appeared in a series of letters written by Alexander Hamilton, James Madison, and John Jay. These were published in newspapers to build popular support for the

Constitution and sway the views of the delegates attending New York State's ratifying convention. Their letters came to be known as the *Federalist Papers*. Combined, these essays provide a comprehensive discussion of how this new government would work to provide greater security and freedom for the nation's citizens.

The authors of the *Federalist Papers* argued that the central government's powers were not nearly as extensive as their opponents suggested. Madison contended that the new government's powers, as granted to Congress in Article I, were "few and defined," with the rest reserved to the states. He argued that because state governments were closer to the people and more likely to have their support and affection, they would be well positioned to restrain any worrisome growth in congressional power.[13] Supporters of the Constitution also argued that the "necessary and proper" clause did not give the Congress a vast reservoir of new powers. As Madison made clear in the *Federalist*, this clause instead only allowed Congress a freedom to choose how enumerated powers would be carried out. The framers of the document, he argued, could not have specified in advance every conceivable means that Congress could take to discharge responsibilities expressly given to it. He also took care to remind his readers that the framers of the Constitution included protections against the abuse of this power. Any congressional effort to use this clause to expand the institution's reach in ways not related to powers enumerated in Article I, Section 8, would be constrained by the other branches of government or checked by the people at the ballot box.[14]

The *Federalist*'s authors also responded to antifederalist complaints that Congress would be too removed from the people and thus not representative of their interests. They addressed this criticism in several different essays. Madison argued that the writers of the Constitution deftly used the selection process and terms of office to increase the likelihood that Congress would include the most qualified and meritorious members of the political class to represent the citizenry. While the antifederalists complained that the size of the House of Representative was too small to represent diverse interests spread across the nation, Madison contended that a smaller-sized House representing larger constituencies would bring forth better qualified candidates "who possess the most attractive merit" to contest the available seats. Madison also believed that to win elections, the candidates would have to be able to demonstrate their talents and skills to a much larger number of voters. At the same time, Madison insisted that House members' two-year terms would be long enough for them to learn their district's needs yet short enough to ensure they would remain accountable to their constituents through elections.[15]

The authors of the *Federalist Papers* realized that House members, because of their shorter terms of office, would be more responsive to public opinion. Given dramatic shifts in public opinion and attitudes, this could lead to instability and frequent changes in law and policy. They worried that too much change and instability would weaken the public's confidence in government. Madison noted the writers of the Constitution anticipated this problem of instability in government when they designed the Senate, a body composed of members indirectly elected by state legislatures for six-year terms. This longer term would provide the legislative branch with greater stability and continuity than a much shorter term would offer. It would also give senators the opportunity to become more familiar with their constituents' needs and problems and more knowledgeable about the "objects and principles of legislation." This would ensure better decisions by the legislative body as a whole. Madison also believed that, along with indirect election by state legislatures, a longer term would provide senators more independence and free them from having to worry about responding to the popular impulses and passions that might hold sway over their House colleagues. The Senate would therefore be an important restraining or moderating force. Moreover, by requiring that these two distinct chambers agree on legislation before sending it to the president, Madison believed that it would be difficult for Congress to expand its reach in ways that would threaten the liberties of individual citizens.[16]

The *Federalist*'s authors also circled back to an important theme raised during the convention's deliberations. This theme involved designing governmental institutions and their relations with one another to prevent abuses of power. Supporters of the Constitution were realistic enough to understand that all governments, including the one designed in Philadelphia, ultimately depend on human beings to exercise power. As they frankly admitted, even the most virtuous citizens could not always be trusted to seek and advance the common good of the community at the expense of their own narrower concerns. The writers of the *Federalist Papers* agreed. "If men were angels," Madison wrote, "no government would be necessary. If angels were to govern men, neither external nor internal controls on government would be necessary. In framing a government that is to be administered by men over men, the great difficulty lies in this: You must first enable the government to control the governed; and in the next place oblige it to control itself." Madison concluded that this was best done by putting in place "auxiliary precautions" or backup measures, to check the abuse of power by governmental officeholders.[17]

Madison maintained that one such precautionary measure to limit the abuse of power was the size of the republic itself. The authors of the *Federalist Papers* believed that the number and diversity of interests that such a large republic included, and the competition between them that it would generate, would make it difficult for any one group or "faction" to seize control of the national policy agenda. This would afford lawmakers greater freedom in their deliberations to advance the good of the entire community when they carried out their legislative responsibilities. The other safeguard against governmental abuse involved a system of checks and balances. As Madison noted, the framers of the Constitution had designed governmental institutions to make it difficult for any one of the branches, and especially the legislature, to consolidate its power. In particular, Madison argued that their goal was to give the occupants of the different institutions of government—Congress, the executive, and the judiciary—the incentives and constitutional means to counter one another.[18] That system of checks and balances, combined with free elections, would prevent this new government from threatening the people's liberties, as the antifederalists feared.

In the end, the supporters of the Constitution prevailed. There were more of them, they were better prepared, and they made their case more effectively. Still, even though they won the day and managed to get the new Constitution approved, they had to agree to add a statement of individual rights to the Constitution after the new government went into effect in 1789. That was the price to be paid to put them over the finish line. The addition of these rights occupied the attention of the first Congress. That body approved twelve amendments to the Constitution. These were sent to the states, which ratified all but two of them. These ten amendments, known as the Bill of Rights, provided additional constraints on Congress and the rest of the government. The first amendment specifically singles out Congress and holds that it may not enact legislation abridging religious freedoms, freedom of expression and assembly, or the right to petition the government. The other amendments provide guarantees with respect to citizens' other liberties and freedoms, and many of these also impose limits on congressional power.

NOTES

1. Donald A. Ritchie, *The U.S. Congress: A Very Short Introduction* (New York: Oxford University Press, 2016), 1–23; and David Brian Robertson, *The Original Compromise: What the Constitution's Framers Were Really Thinking* (New York: Oxford University Press, 2013), 44.

2. Richard Beeman, *Plain, Honest Men: The Making of the American Constitution* (New York: Random House, 2009), 106.

3. Robertson, *The Original Compromise*, 44.

4. Anthony King, *The Founding Fathers v. The People: Perspectives of American Democracy* (Cambridge, MA: Harvard University Press, 2012), 44.

5. Beeman, *Plain, Honest Men*, 110–11.

6. Jack N. Rakove, "From the Old Congress to the New," in *The American Congress: The Building of Democracy*, ed. Julian E. Zelizer (New York: Houghton Mifflin Company, 2004), 16–18.

7. Beeman, *Plain, Honest Men*, 289–90.

8. Robertson, *The Original Compromise*, 43.

9. Robertson, *The Original Compromise*, 117.

10. Herbert J. Storing, *What the Anti-Federalists Were For* (Chicago: University of Chicago Press, 1981), 15–23.

11. Rakove, "From the Old Congress to the New," 20.

12. Rakove, "From the Old Congress to the New," 20–21; Samuel Bryan, "Centinel," in *The Debate on the Constitution*, ed. Bernard Bailyn, 2 vols. (New York: Library of America, 1993), 1:61.

13. James Madison, *Federalist No. 45*, in *Debate on the Constitution*, 2:105–6.

14. Madison, *Federalist No. 44*, 2:93–100.

15. Madison, *Federalist No.10*, 1:409–10.

16. Madison, *Federalist No. 62*, 2:244–50.

17. Madison, *Federalist No. 51*, 2:164–65.

18. Madison, *Federalist No. 10*, 1:410; and Madison, *Federalist No. 51*, 2:163–67.

2

Congressional Change

At the convention, the founders spent considerable time designing Congress and determining its powers and relations with the other branches of government. Still, when they wrote the Constitution, they provided few details on how it would be organized and work. They did not even mention many of the most important features we associate with Congress today. The Constitution says nothing about many of its rules and procedures. It includes no references to congressional committees or political parties, even though both have been central to legislative work since the earliest years of the republic. There is also no mention of the congressional staff or aides who play an important role assisting congressional committees and members of Congress, either on Capitol Hill or in lawmakers' district and state offices.

As experienced politicians and serious students of government, the framers recognized that they needed to provide flexibility so that Congress could adapt to the historical changes they expected but could not fully anticipate. They therefore left many decisions on congressional organization and procedures to those who would serve as legislators themselves. Over time, lawmakers have used that leverage to bring about important institutional changes.

CONGRESSIONAL ORGANIZATION AND PROCEDURES

The Constitution gives members of Congress great leeway over how they organize their chambers. Article I provides for congressional officers but says little about their roles and responsibilities. It gives the House the power to choose its own Speaker. Still, it provides no specific clues about what the Speaker should do. It also sets no qualifications for the office. It does not even say that the Speaker must be an elected representative, though all who have served in that position have been. The Constitution also gives House members the authority to establish and fill any other offices they deem necessary, but it is silent on organizational matters beyond that.

The Constitution is only slightly more explicit when it comes to the Senate's officers. It specifies that the vice president of the United States shall be the president of the Senate, but it only gives the vice president the power to cast a tie-breaking vote when the chamber is "equally divided." It neither invites nor prohibits the vice president's involvement in chamber deliberations and debates. The Constitution also calls on senators to elect a president pro tempore to fill in when the vice president is unavailable to serve, though it says little else about the position. As is the case with the House, it leaves senators free to create and fill additional offices as they see fit.

The Constitution provides some direction to congressional work. It says Congress must meet at least once each year, and it prevents either house from adjourning without the consent of the other for longer than three days or moving to another place without the other's consent. It states that each of the two chambers must have a quorum—a majority of its members—to conduct business. The Constitution also requires Congress to keep records of its work. It says, for instance, that each chamber must maintain a journal of its proceedings and publish it "from time to time" and that votes on "any questions" in either house must be recorded in the journal at the request of one-fifth of its members. It also specifies that certain actions require a supermajority vote of two-thirds of the members. Both chambers need such a supermajority to override a presidential veto of legislation and to initiate an amendment to the Constitution, and the Senate needs one to ratify treaties and convict officials impeached by the House of Representatives. In addition, the Constitution requires a two-thirds vote of either house to expel any one of its members.

The Constitution outlines lawmaking procedures in Article I, Section 7. It says that all bills raising revenue—that is, tax legislation—must "originate" in the House of Representatives. It also says that before a specific bill can become law, it must first be adopted by both houses of Congress and then must be presented to the president of the United States for approval. In addition, it describes what the legislative body can do if the president chooses to veto legislation. Yet it provides little direction beyond that. The section says nothing about how laws should be drafted or how they should be taken for up consideration, debated, and voted on. While it says that before a bill can become law it must be adopted by each chamber, it provides no clues as to how the House and the Senate should resolve their differences on a bill that passes the two chambers in different forms. The framers instead left these types of procedural decisions to Congress itself by inserting in the Constitution a clause that authorizes "each House to determine the Rules of its proceedings."

While the Constitution specifies the powers and responsibilities of Congress and imposes limits on its powers, it still leaves lawmakers with great control over how they organize themselves and conduct business. Legislators, in turn, have used that rather substantial authority to develop rules, procedures, norms, strategies, and structures of leadership to help them meet their responsibilities. Today's Congress is the result of the many changes made by lawmakers as they have adapted the institution to respond to the social, economic, and political changes that periodically sweep across the American political landscape.

DEVELOPMENT OF CONGRESS: THE FIRST CENTURY

Very few of those individuals elected to Congress prior to the end of the nineteenth century viewed service in the institution as a career. Most of them were only part-time lawmakers. They usually combined their service in Congress with their work as lawyers, merchants, or farmers. Members frequently arrived at sessions late or left early so that they could tend to their business affairs and family back home. This often left them short of a quorum. Membership turnover was common. Representatives rarely stayed beyond a term or two, while many senators resigned their positions well before their six-year terms were up. They had few incentives to stay or seek reelection. Some found political affairs back home more appealing. Because the national government had limited responsibilities, many important decisions were still made back in their state legislatures, not in the nation's capital. Many senators and representatives didn't especially like the work and found the travel of the job difficult and time-consuming.

Once the center of government permanently relocated to Washington, DC, in 1800, they had another reason not to stay around. Compared to the previous seats of the central government, New York and Philadelphia, their new capital city was small, dingy, and unattractive. Its climate was insufferable much of the year. Their living quarters provided little privacy and few comforts, as most members had to reside in cramped boardinghouses while tending to their official duties. The Capitol building in which they worked was under construction through long stretches of time during the nineteenth century, making it difficult for legislators to go about their chores. Many also found Washington dull, a city with a bland social life and few cultural refinements.[1]

Of course, many able and even notable politicians answered the call for congressional service during its first century of existence. But the institution also drew to its chambers lawmakers of limited talents and questionable character. Many of them were crude, undisciplined, and uninformed. Some were also easily corrupted. Unending and chaotic debates, rude behavior, personal insults, and threats were not uncommon. Congressional proceedings were frequently disorderly and tumultuous, while legislative debates reflected deep personal and political conflicts that occasionally erupted into bouts of violence and bloodshed.

Still, even in these years leading up to the Civil War and Reconstruction, Congress put into place practices and structures that helped it meet its responsibilities and adapt to the needs of a growing American republic. It thus established a foundation that succeeding generations of lawmakers would build on to shape it into the institution that we see today. First, the members of Congress asserted control over their proceedings and thus established important procedures and precedents for how the chambers would carry out their work. Second, they developed two important organizational structures—the aforementioned political parties and committees—that have been central to legislative life and work.

Congress took a series of actions important for its future development when it first convened in March 1789. Both chambers asserted control over their internal procedures. They adopted rules to guide their work and created and filled administrative positions. The House elected its first Speaker and set down that office's duties. These included presiding over floor debates, making decisions on parliamentary decisions, casting a vote only to break ties, and serving as the chamber's symbolic and administrative leader. The workings and evolution of the House eventually made it difficult for the Speaker to stay above the fray of partisan politics, but the expectation that the Speaker be charged with overseeing the institution still holds true.

Meanwhile, relations between members of the Senate and Vice President John Adams set expectations for the institution's presiding officer. After coming under criticism for injecting himself in some of the Senate's early discussions and deliberations, Adams turned to a more limited role of presiding over the chamber, maintaining order, preserving decorum, and casting tie-breaking votes, a script that would be followed by vice presidents until the early 1960s. His immediate successor, Vice President Thomas Jefferson, used some of his time as president of the Senate to write a manual on parliamentary procedures to guide the chamber. The House would incorporate Jefferson's manual into its own rules several years later.[2]

Congress also took an important step in the republic's early days by opening its proceedings to the public. While the Senate initially followed the Articles of Confederation's Continental Congress's practice of conducting its business in secrecy, the House of Representatives agreed almost from the start to let the public watch directly as it went about its legislative business. With the House's proceedings open to the people, the Senate came under increasing political pressure to follow suit. Senators eventually relented, opening their chamber doors to the public in 1795.

Even though the framers disliked political parties or factions and purposely designed their new government to make it hard for them to gain power, parties quickly emerged. They developed as coalitions of lawmakers took sides on political and policy debates that appeared just as the new government was getting off the ground. On one side were Secretary of Treasury Alexander Hamilton and his congressional allies, many of whom came from the more industrial states from the Northeast. They wanted to expand the central government's role and use its powers to promote the nation's manufacturing industries, trade, and economic development. These lawmakers referred to themselves as Federalists. On the other side were Secretary of State Thomas Jefferson and James Madison, a leading House member in the early Congress. They were supported by lawmakers who came from the country's more agrarian regions. To set them apart from their opponents, they identified themselves as Democratic-Republicans. They opposed Hamilton's economic proposals and his call to expand the central government's role. They instead wanted to keep more power in the hands of state and local government officials.

The two sides' political leaders worked through these emerging legislative parties to advance their political and policy goals. Hamilton frequently lobbied his Federalist allies in Congress to support his ambitious economic plans. Meanwhile, Jefferson worked behind the scenes and enlisted Madison to work with Democratic-Republican colleagues to plot out legislative strategies to block Hamilton's proposals. Leaders on both sides thus used informal networks of legislators to build coalitions, share information, and put pressure on members to support their positions. Their strategies and actions marked the beginning of a congressional party system.

This first party system changed as the founding generation's politicians passed from the scene. After suffering several electoral defeats, the Federalist Party gradually disintegrated. Still, many of its ideas lived on. They were picked up by a new generation of politicians who formed the Whig Party. At the same time, with the election of Andrew Jackson, supporters of Democratic-Republican principles began to identify themselves simply as Democrats. Like the Federalists and Democratic-Republicans before them, these two parties contested elections and competed with one another within Congress. Conflicts over slavery and secession eventually produced deep rifts in the Whig Party. Unable to manage its internal divisions, the party fell apart and a new political party, the Grand Old Party or Republican Party, emerged in the mid-1850s to take its place. Yet these changes did not diminish the role that parties played in congressional activities. Though absent from the Constitution, they had become the primary vehicles that lawmakers used to organize their chambers, select their leaders, build coalitions, pass legislation, and work out relations with the executive branch. Furthermore, by the start of the civil war, Democrats and Republicans were firmly in place. These two parties have dominated congressional activities in the United States ever since.

Legislative committees also emerged as parties started to take hold in Congress. Initially, members in each chamber met as a committee of the whole to legislate. To resolve thorny problems that hampered their work, the House and the Senate created ad hoc or temporary committees. Once a temporary committee finished its task and reported back to the full chamber, it was disbanded. Because of its larger membership, the House soon learned this was not a good way to proceed. Involving so many people in writing legislation and creating committees when legislative problems emerged proved to be unwieldy, time-consuming, and frustrating, and it put the institution at a disadvantage in dealing with the White House. This was also especially troubling for the House because it was the center of much of the nation's legislative activity.

Its members responded to these problems by gradually creating standing or permanent committees. It gave each standing committee authority over a specific set of policies or issues. Standing-committee members assumed responsibility for learning about the issues that fell within their committee's domain and gained the power to review and modify legislation before they referred it to all House members for debate and a vote.

The Senate lagged behind the House in creating permanent committees. Some of this was due to its smaller size, which made it easier for that legislative body to conduct business. Yet within a few years, the Senate, too, found that it needed specialized permanent committees to accomplish its work, so it adopted rules that put them in place. By the time that James Monroe took office as the fifth president of the United States in 1817, both chambers routinely relied on permanent legislative committees.[3]

The House played the leading role in the earliest years of the republic. With Madison informally leading the chamber during its opening session, the House spearheaded the drive to write and approve a series of amendments to the Constitution that Congress sent to the states for their ratification. The ten amendments that the states approved came to be known as the Bill of Rights. The House also took the lead in creating the different offices of the government and in funding their operations. During these early years, it developed a reputation as the more attractive of the two chambers. Henry Clay of Kentucky, who was elected Speaker on his first day in office in 1811, showed how a skilled politician could use that office to control the institution and shape national policy to fuel his ambition to seek the presidency. Yet within a few years after parties and committees were firmly established, the Senate moved to center stage. It became more desirable as the size of the House increased with the growth in the nation's population.[4] The smaller size of the Senate gave individual members greater prominence, thus making it more attractive to politicians with ambitions for other national offices, such as the presidency. Several leading House members, including Henry Clay, were elected to the Senate by their state legislatures. There they attracted attention as they debated and negotiated compromises on highly visible and complicated issues, including the spread and continuation of slavery.

CONGRESS IN THE AGE OF INDUSTRIALIZATION

Congress witnessed change and addressed new challenges in the decades between the Civil War and the start of the twentieth century.[5] The post–Civil War era brought important changes in congressional membership. Political reforms enacted during Reconstruction initially produced a more diverse congressional membership. In addition to abolishing slavery, extending citizenship, and providing equality under the law to former slaves, reformers granted African American men the right to vote. Many of them used their newly gained power at the ballot box to elect African Americans to public office. As a result, in the early post–Civil War years, several southern states included African Americans—all Republicans—in their congressional delegations.

This trend proved to be short lived, however. Once Reconstruction ended, white southerners regained political power. Once they reasserted control of their state and local governments, they used measures and tactics, including assault and murder, to keep African Americans from voting. This resulted in a collapse of the number of minority lawmakers. Shortly after the turn of the twentieth century, none were left. Another African American was not elected to Congress for almost three more decades.

A second change in congressional membership, though less immediately noticeable, was more durable. As the nation became more industrialized and the role of the central government grew, the job of a lawmaker became more important and challenging. By the end of the century, most congressional offices even included a small staff. A congressional career was much more inviting than it had been in the past. The number of lawmakers who sought and successfully gained reelection increased. This produced a decline in membership turnover. Lawmakers stayed longer, and they amassed more experience than their predecessors. This trend of making a career of congressional service continued through the rest of the twentieth century and still holds true today.

The decline in membership turnover coincided with a significant increase in partisanship on Capitol Hill (often referred to simply as "the Hill"). From the 1890s through the first years of the twentieth century, the two parties, Democrats and Republicans, were sharply divided from one another. They differed greatly in their beliefs on how the power of the national government should be used, and they waged contentious battles within Congress to shape policy outcomes. Bipartisan cooperation was rare. Instead, members of the same political party stuck together when they wrote, debated, and voted on legislation, and their leaders started exercising more power to help them achieve their partisan goals.

In 1899, both parties in the House created new, formal leadership officers—House majority leader and House minority leader—to coordinate their operations and maintain party discipline in floor proceedings and votes. Yet the majority party had an important advantage in the centralization of power. Because it controlled what happened in the House, it effectively picked the Speaker and used its control of the rules to help the Speaker centralize power in his hands. By the turn of the twentieth century, the Speaker had gained almost unilateral control over committee assignments and the chamber's operations. The Speaker at the time, Republican representative Joseph Cannon from Illinois, was so powerful and had so much leverage over the House's procedures that members frequently described him as a "czar," a political figure vested with great power.

Distribution of power in the Senate differed from that in the House. Because of its smaller size and less restrictive rules, individual senators had much more leverage in their chamber. This was as true then as it is today. Protective of their powers, senators were less inclined to support strong leaders. They instead relied on an informal leadership network that had been in place since the turn of the century. It consisted of a small group of influential senators who stepped forward to organize and guide the work of their parties. They applied their expertise and parliamentary and negotiating skills to influence committee assignments, shape the Senate's legislative agenda, and direct proceedings and floor debates.[6] As a result, the Senate lagged behind the House in creating formal party leadership offices. Senate Democrats did not establish an official floor leader until 1920, and Republicans did not create one until 1925.

THE COMMITTEE-CENTERED CONGRESS

The rise of an early twentieth-century political movement known as progressivism spurred more change on Capitol Hill. Progressives fought for and gained many political and economic reforms. They wanted to wrest political power away from special interests in society and to expand democracy.

They also wanted to use government to regulate the large powerful corporations and economic trusts that emerged during the era of industrialization. These reformers took their fight to Washington, DC, as well as to state and local governments. Running on campaigns promising reform, several of them also got elected to Congress, where they pushed for significant changes in the nation's policies. Since several of them were prominent Republicans from midwestern states, their election to Congress brought greater political diversity to their party. The party now had a progressive wing as well as an economically conservative one.

One important progressive political reform that had a direct impact on Congress was the adoption of the Seventeenth Amendment in 1913. This change to the Constitution took away state legislatures' power to select senators. It gave that power to the voters. This meant that going forward, senators had to appeal directly to the people at the ballot box, just as their House colleagues were required to do. A second significant political reform expanded the franchise and helped touch off a change in the composition of Congress. Many progressives added their weight to the women's suffrage movement. In 1920, the movement finally reached its goal by securing congressional passage and state ratification of the Nineteenth Amendment. This addition to the Constitution gave women the right to vote. It also led to change on the Hill, as a small number of women started to contest and win elections to Congress.[7]

Shortly after the start of the twentieth century, reformers within both congressional parties also pushed for policies that promised to check the abuses of corporate power. Early on, they found an important ally in President Theodore Roosevelt, who vigorously and publicly advanced their reform agenda. With his encouragement and support, they introduced several measures that sought to curb large corporations' hold on the economy. Speaker Cannon opposed these initiatives and for a time blocked their efforts. An economic conservative, he did not support most progressive policies, and he used his formidable powers to prevent their legislation from even being taken up for consideration in committees.

Shortly after the more economically conservative William Howard Taft succeeded Roosevelt to the presidency, however, progressives within the majority Republican Party rebelled, having grown weary of Cannon's heavy-handed opposition to their reform agenda and the Taft administration's more conservative policy stance. They joined forces with the Democrats and gained control of the chamber in 1910. In order to move forward with their reforms, they took away many of Speaker Cannon's powers, stripping that office of its ability to single-handedly kill their legislative initiatives. This created an opening for them to begin making many important social and economic reforms that also expanded the role played by the central government.[8]

Following the revolt against Cannon and the weakening of the speaker-ship, congressional parties started losing some of their influence. Splits within each of the parties appeared, and partisanship declined. Members started crossing the aisle from time to time to work with the lawmakers from the opposing party. This was especially the case for the Democrats. Southern Democrats elected to Congress were more conservative than their northern colleagues. They were also less loyal and much more inclined to vote with the Republicans on many policy issues that threatened to undermine their control of southern politics, especially on issues of race. Together, they formed a conservative coalition of lawmakers that remained a formidable alliance within Congress for the next half century.

This decline in party loyalties coincided with a change in the distribu-tion of power on Capitol Hill.[9] Standing committees became even more important and influential. They effectively controlled the fate of bills over which they had jurisdiction. They determined which bills would be taken up for consideration, they wrote the legislation, and they determined when and how it would be considered on the floor. They often had the power to determine whether a proposal had a chance to be enacted into law. Other members in the chamber usually deferred to the committees' recommen-dations when they made their own decisions on legislation.

Congress developed unwritten rules or norms that guided committee members' behaviors. These norms directed members to specialize in one or two issues within their committees and to carry out their work without a lot of fanfare or publicity. They also encouraged members to defer to their more senior colleagues on their committees. Lawmakers quickly learned that if they wanted to advance in their congressional careers and have an impact within their committees and on the legislative process, they needed to comply with these norms to gain support within the institution.

As committees' leverage increased, so did the influence of those who led them. To avoid infighting over who would chair these powerful bod-ies, congressional parties increasingly relied on the informal rule or norm of seniority. Parties determined seniority by counting consecutive years of service on the committee. The most senior member of the majority party on the committee automatically became the chair, while the most senior member of the minority party became the ranking member. Con-gressional committee chairs' power had many sources. They had years of experience and a wealth of knowledge and had accumulated staff mem-bers to help them with their work. This gave them an edge over others. Congressional rules also put them in charge of committee operations and committee meetings, which were frequently held behind closed doors, away from the press and the public. They controlled their committee's staff resources and had the most say over legislation it considered. Others, especially those in their own party, deferred to them when it came to floor deliberations, proceedings, and votes. The committee chairs also carried out negotiations on legislation with the president and cut deals with their counterparts in the other chamber to work out differences on bills that had passed both bodies.

By the 1930s, committee chairs had consolidated power on the Hill. Even congressional party leaders like the Speaker had to bargain and cut deals with them to get things done in Congress. Although committee chairs confronted challenges in their legislative work and did not always prevail, they became so influential that many started referring to them as the "barons" of Congress. They remained the most important members of Congress through the 1960s and early 1970s.

THE REFORM CONGRESS

Committee chairs started to come under pressure beginning in the 1960s. Elections in those years brought to Congress many lawmakers who quickly grew exasperated and angry with committee chairs' exercise of power. Frustration mounted, especially on the Democratic side of the aisle. They had large majorities in both chambers through much of the post–World War II era. Yet many of their committee chairs came from the South, a region the Democratic Party had dominated since the end of the Civil War. Meanwhile, many of these newly elected Democrats came from the North. They were more liberal than the senior southern Democrats who, because of the norm of seniority, had managed to gain control of many of the standing committees in Congress. These southern Democratic committee chairs used their power to thwart and effectively kill legislation favored by their more liberal counterparts in the party. Many of their more junior and more liberal Democratic colleagues grew impatient as they saw the southern bloc of their party delay, dilute, and defeat their efforts to remove barriers to civil rights, fight poverty, and support urban development. They were unhappy with the pace of change and their inability to play a bigger role in the legislative process. They sought a more immediate impact on what Congress did and were less inclined to play by the old rules.

As their ranks grew over time, these more junior Democratic members pushed to reform Congress. After gaining more influence within their party, which had control of both chambers on the Hill, they finally got it to adopt several reforms.[10] They trimmed committee chairs' powers. They delegated more authority to subcommittees and strengthened the hand of those who led them. They implemented reforms that opened committees' proceedings to the public and the press. They weakened the norm of seniority for choosing committee chairs. These more junior lawmakers also sought and successfully obtained an increase in staff support for the institution to provide them with the professional expertise they needed to make important legislative and policy decisions. They likewise provided themselves with large increases in office personnel to support their operations back home in their state and districts as well as their legislative work on the Hill. Finally, many of them refused to play by the informal rules that had long held sway in Washington. As these norms gave way, more members gained the freedom to play an increased role in the legislative process and to do so at a much earlier stage in their careers.

By the end of the 1970s, Congress was a noticeably different place. It was no longer an institution where small groups of lawmakers led by powerful chairs could manage and control its work as they bargained with one another behind closed doors. Instead, power in Congress was more evenly distributed. The institution now made more of its decisions in public and frequently conducted much of its work in front of television cameras. Regular members, often called rank-and-file members, had more resources and leverage. They were also far more inclined to use these newly acquired resources and influence for their own goals as the informal norms that regulated congressional behavior fell by the wayside. Congress became more individualistic and freewheeling as more and more members got directly involved in shaping policy outcomes. This made it hard for congressional parties to keep their members in line and get things done.

THE CONTEMPORARY CONGRESS

During the early 1980s Congress began to evolve into the more partisan and politically divided institution that exists today.[11] This happened as it adapted to transformations on the larger political landscape. The most important was the change in the electorate's voting patterns. Beginning in the late 1960s and continuing through the early 1980s, many southern and a few western states started electing Republicans to Congress. They replaced the more conservative Democrats who had once held those seats and left office. As the number of conservative Democratic lawmakers declined, so did the divisions within the party. Congressional Democrats found themselves agreeing with one another more often.

While this was unfolding, something similar was happening to congressional Republicans. Voters replaced several moderate Republicans from primarily northeastern and northwestern states with Democrats. This decline in the number of moderate and liberal Republicans produced a more united and conservative Republican Party. Combined, these changes led to significant increases in party loyalty on the Hill and an increase in the differences between the parties. Bipartisanship, or a willingness to cross party lines, declined as a result. By the end of the 1990s, the two parties had become sharply divided and opposed to one another in their policy preferences on virtually all the major issues of the day. The most liberal Republicans in Congress were generally more conservative than the most conservative Democrats, something that is still the case today. Because of this polarization, relations between the two parties have become increasingly contentious and confrontational.

In this more partisan environment, each of the congressional parties has turned to its leaders to help it achieve its own party goals. This is especially true in the House of Representatives, though both parties also expect their Senate leaders to exercise greater influence. To that end, congressional parties have strengthened their leaders' hands, and Hill leaders have taken up the call. They now play a greater role in managing their parties' congressional operations than they have at any point in the last one hundred years. They have a strong say in influencing committee assignments, shaping the congressional agenda, and managing the legislative process. They also raise money for congressional elections, and they recruit and aggressively work to elect their party's candidates to congressional office. In addition, they have assumed the important responsibilities of being the principal spokespersons for their parties, communicating their parties' messages to the public, and helping their members use the media to that end as well.

Today's congressional parties are as partisan and divided as they were more than a century ago. Politics on the Hill are divisive and contentious, and relations with the executive and judicial branches are frequently strained. Even under the best of conditions, when a single party controls both chambers of Congress as well as the presidency, it is difficult to get things done. And when the chambers of Congress and the presidency fall into the hands of different parties, producing what is known as divided government, stalemate or gridlock is often the result. That is arguably one of the reasons why people's approval of Congress has plummeted to near record lows in recent years.

NOTES

1. Benjamin Ginsberg and Kathryn Wagner Hill, *Congress: The First Branch* (New Haven, CT: Yale University Press, 2019); Robert V. Remini, *The House: The History of the House of Representatives* (New York: HarperCollins, 2007); Joanne B. Freeman, *The Field of Blood: Violence in Congress and the Road to Civil War* (New York: Farrar, Straus and Giroux, 2018); James Sterling Young, *The Washington Community: 1800–1828* (New York: Harcourt Brace Jovanovich, 1966); and Joanne Barrie Freeman, "Opening Congress," in *The American Congress: The Building of Democracy*, ed. Julian E. Zelizer (New York: Houghton Mifflin, 2004), 25–37.

2. Ronald M. Peters Jr., *The American Speakership: The Office in Historical Perspective* (Baltimore, MD: Johns Hopkins Press, 1997), chap. 1; Freeman, "Opening Congress"; and U.S. Senate, "John Adams, 1st Vice President (1789–1797)," accessed June 27, 2020, https://www.senate.gov/about/officers-staff/vice-president/VP_John_Adams.htm.

3. Eric Schickler, "Institutional Development of Congress," in *The Legislative Branch*, eds. Paul Quirk and Sarah Binder (New York: Oxford University Press, 2005), 35–62.

4. Neil MacNeil and Richard Baker, *The American Senate: An Insider's History* (New York: Oxford University Press, 2013), chaps. 6 and 11.

5. Information on discussion of congressional change during this era draws upon the following: E. Scott Adler, Jeffery A. Jenkins, and Charles R. Shipan, *The United States Congress* (New York: W. W. Norton, 2019), chap. 2; Eric Rauchway, "The Transformation of the Congressional Experience," in *The American Congress: The Building of Democracy*, ed. Julian E. Zelizer (New York: Houghton Mifflin, 2004), 319–33; Schickler, "Institutional Development of Congress"; Peters, *American Speakership*; Ginsberg and Hill, *Congress*, chap. 2; MacNeil and Baker, *American Senate*, chap. 7; and Randall P. Ripley, *Power in the Senate* (New York: St. Martin's Press, 1969).

6. MacNeil and Baker, *American Senate*, chap. 7.

7. David Kyvig, "Redesigning Congress: The Seventeenth and Twentieth Amendments to the Constitution," in *The American Congress: The Building of Democracy*, ed. Julian E. Zelizer (New York: Houghton Mifflin, 2004), 356–69; Alison B. Parker, "Women's Activism," in *The American Congress: The Building of Democracy*, ed. Julian E. Zelizer (New York: Houghton Mifflin, 2004), 370–94.

8. Elizabeth Sanders, "Economic Regulation in the Progressive Era," in *The American Congress: The Building of Democracy*, ed. Julian E. Zelizer (New York: Houghton Mifflin, 2004), 337–50; Remini, *House*, chap. 11; and Peters, *American Speakership*, chap. 2.

9. For a discussion on the committee-dominated era that followed, see James L. Sundquist, *The Decline and Resurgence of Congress* (Washington, DC: Brookings Institution, 1981); Ronald Brownstein, *The Second Civil War: How Extreme Partisanship Has Paralyzed Washington and Polarized America* (New York: Penguin Press, 2007), esp. chap. 5; James MacGregor Burns, *Congress on Trial: The Legislative Process and the Administrative State* (New York: Harper and Brothers, 1949); Nelson Polsby, *How Congress Evolves: Social Bases of Institutional Change* (Oxford: Oxford University Press, 2004); Leroy N. Rieselbach, *Congressional Reform: The Changing Modern Congress* (Washington, DC: Congressional Quarterly Press, 1994); Herbert B. Asher, "The Learning of Legislative Norms," *American Political Science Review* 67 (June 1973): 499–513; Norman Ornstein, "The Open Congress Meets the President," in *Both Ends of the Avenue: The Presidency, the Executive Branch, and Congress in the 1980s*, ed. Anthony King (Washington, DC: American Enterprise Institute for Public Policy Research, 1983), 185–211; Donald R. Matthews, *U.S. Senators and Their World* (Chapel Hill: University of North Carolina Press, 1960); and K. A. Shepsle, "The Changing Textbook Congress," in *Can the Government Govern?*, eds. J. E. Chubb and P. E. Peterson (Washington, DC: Brookings Institution, 1989).

10. The reforms and their effects on Congress are discussed in Roger H. Davidson, "Subcommittee Government: New Channels of Policymaking," in *The New Congress*, eds. Thomas E. Mann and Norman J. Ornstein (Washington, DC: American Enterprise Institute for Public Policy Research, 1981); Polsby, *How Congress Evolves*; Rieselbach, *Congressional Reform*; Julian Zelizer, *On Capitol Hill: The Struggle to Reform Congress and Its Consequences* (Cambridge: Cambridge University Press, 2004); Eric Schickler, *Disjointed Pluralism: Institutional Innovation and the Development of the U.S. Congress* (Princeton, NJ: Princeton University Press, 2001), chap. 5; and Samuel C. Patterson, "The Semi-Sovereign Congress," in *The New American Political System*, ed. Anthony King (Washington, DC: American Enterprise Institute for Public Policy Research, 1978), 125–78.

11. See Steven S. Smith and Gerald Gamm, "The Dynamics of Party Government in Congress," in *Congress Reconsidered*, eds. Lawrence C. Dodd and Bruce I. Oppenheimer (Washington, DC: CQ Press, 2005), 185–201; David Rohde, *Parties and Leaders in the Postreform House* (Chicago: University of Chicago Press, 1991); Gary Jacobson, "Party Polarization in National Politics: The Electoral Connection," in *Polarized Politics: Congress and the President in a Partisan Era*, eds. Jon R. Bond and Richard Fleisher (Washington, DC: CQ Press, 2000), 9–30; Bruce I. Oppenheimer, "Deep Red and Blue Congressional Districts: The Causes and Consequences of Declining Party Competitiveness," in *Congress Reconsidered*, eds. Lawrence C. Dodd and Bruce I. Oppenheimer (Washington, DC: CQ Press, 2005), 135–58; Paul Quirk, "The Legislative Branch: Assessing the Partisan Congress," in *A Republic Divided, The Annenberg Democracy Project*, eds. Paul Quirk and Sarah Binder (New York: Oxford University Press, 2007), 130–31; Barbara Sinclair, "Parties and Leadership in the House," in *The Legislative Branch*, eds. Paul J. Quirk and Sarah A. Binder (New York: Oxford University Press, 2005), 224–54; and Barbara Sinclair, *Legislators, Leaders, and Lawmaking: The U.S. House of Representatives in the Postreform Era* (Baltimore, MD: Johns Hopkins University Press, 1995).

3

Congressional Campaigns and Elections

Elections are at the heart of congressional politics, touching virtually every aspect of the institution. They reflect the legislature's constitutional design and are the doorways that link Congress to the citizenry. Apart from appointments to the Senate when an unexpected vacancy occurs, everyone in Congress first had to win an election. The types of campaigns run by those who want to serve are determined by forces that shape the larger political landscape. These include the issues that capture the imagination and awaken the passions of the American people as well as changes in political parties, society, the economy, and communication technologies. Elections periodically send new kinds of politicians with distinctive characteristics and goals to Capitol Hill, which in turn leads to changes in how the institution operates. Studying congressional elections thus helps us understand both who gets elected and why, and how these electoral contests are intertwined with these other features of the American political order.

CONGRESSIONAL ELECTIONS AND THE CONSTITUTION

The Constitution provides the framework for congressional elections. Article I requires the entire House and one-third of the Senate to stand for election every two years, and it sets age, citizenship, and residency requirements for both chambers. Senators need to be at least thirty years old when they take office. They must also have been a U.S. citizen for at least nine years and live in the state in which they are running for election. House members need to be at least twenty-five years old when they take office, have been a U.S. citizen for at least seven years, and reside in the state that includes the district they will represent. They do not have to live in the district itself, though living in a different district can raise political challenges come election time. On the day of a special House election in Georgia in 2017, for example, President Donald Trump tweeted that the Democratic candidate did not reside in the district he hoped to represent. The candidate admitted that was true, acknowledging he lived with his girlfriend who lived in the adjoining district. She was a medical student at Emory University, and they lived there so that she could walk to school. By one count, twenty-one House members lived outside of the district that elected them in 2017, including seven Republican members. In every case the representatives, like the Democratic candidate mentioned above, lived right next door to their districts.[1] For all practical purposes, representatives reside among those who send them to Congress.

The framers set the Constitution's election requirements with specific purposes in mind. The age qualifications ensure legislators have broad life experience, and the residency requirements increase the chances that members are familiar with their constituents' interests. The citizenship provisions reflect the framers' efforts to keep elections free from foreign interference while still encouraging immigration by giving relatively new arrivals the chance to hold government office. As James Madison put it, apart from these qualifications, the framers wanted the legislative body to be "open to merit of every description, whether native or adoptive, whether young or old, and without regard to poverty, wealth, or any particular profession of religious faith."[2]

Election requirements established by the framers help explain what political scientist Richard Fenno identified as a paradox of congressional politics.[3] As the country's legislature, Congress is charged with creating policies that serve the national interest. Yet its members represent specific geographic localities, and to stay in office, they must please the voters in their districts and states. As noted in the introduction, despite long-standing complaints that Congress is filled with members who attend to special interests because all they want to do is get reelected, those raising that complaint keep sending the same people back to the Hill.

One way to make sense of this apparent inconsistency is to recall that the Constitution requires members to represent simultaneously the interests of their constituents and of the entire country. High reelection rates may indicate that most members, most of the time, are especially sensitive to what their constituents want, even as many of those constituents remain unhappy with the institution's overall performance. This dilemma predates the Constitution, as a member who served in an American colonial legislature made clear when he asked "whether a Representative was obliged to follow the directions of his constituents against his own reason and conscience or to be governed by his conscience."[4] Lawmakers, because they are usually rewarded for addressing their own voters' concerns, often respond to this dilemma by taking care of the folks back home. But by doing so, they may make it hard for the institution to advance the national interest, which in turn leads people to complain that the Congress is not doing its job.

INSTITUTIONAL CHANGE AND ELECTIONS: THE FIRST ONE HUNDRED YEARS

Elections from the founding through most of the 1800s differed in several ways from those held today. While representatives have always been elected by the people, the Constitution initially gave state legislatures the power to choose senators. Senate candidates did not join their House colleagues on the campaign trail until the passage of the Seventeenth Amendment in 1913, which called for the direct election of senators.

Moreover, congressional elections were not all held on the same day. States had the discretion to decide when to hold elections for congressional and state offices, and some of them intentionally wanted to separate those contests from the November presidential election. So some members of Congress were elected in the spring of an election year, while others were chosen in the following year. The current practice of holding all congressional elections on the same day has its origins in 1872, when Congress passed a law stating that by 1876, all House and Senate elections would be held every two years on the first Tuesday after the first Monday in November.

Even though many in the founders' generation spoke disapprovingly of political parties, they relied on them right from the start. George Washington's own administration included two figures prominent in the country's first two political parties. They were his secretary of treasury, Alexander Hamilton, who led the Federalist Party, and his secretary of state, Thomas Jefferson, who led the Democratic-Republicans. Members even organized factions or splinter groups within these larger parties to advance their interests through elections. John Randolph, a leading political figure in Virginia, organized and led a movement of like-minded politicians in his state's legislature to deny James Madison a Senate seat. He also worked, unsuccessfully, against Madison's campaign for a House seat.

By the late 1820s, the addition of new states brought increased political pressure to expand the franchise, or the right to vote, and thus gave more citizens the opportunity to participate in elections. The Constitution left the states great leeway in setting the rules that would govern their elections. Initially, states limited the right to vote to white male property owners. This changed as new states joined the Union between 1792 and 1818. Five of the new states came from the less developed western frontier. The sensibilities and economic interests of the inhabitants of those states, which included Kentucky, Tennessee, Ohio, Indiana, and Illinois, differed in some respects from those who resided in the original thirteen states. Many of them gave white men the right to vote even if they did not hold property. This put pressure on the original thirteen states that had property limitations to do away with their restrictions on that score.

The early and sometimes tentative party activities of the founding generation were embraced with more enthusiasm and deployed with more effectiveness by the second generation of Americans. Led by Andrew Jackson and Martin Van Buren, the Democrats emerged in the 1820s as a formidable political force. Their party organizations recruited candidates for state and national office and gave them the resources needed to run effective campaigns. Norms of this era discouraged candidates from speaking on their own behalf, because it might indicate that they were too interested in wielding power and too self-centered to have the public's good in mind. Such behavior was considered unseemly. Parties instead stepped in to make the case for their candidates. Newspapers of the time were partisan, and party leaders and reporters worked together on communication campaigns designed to create a favorable image of their candidates, criticize their political opponents, energize those citizens most likely to support them at the polls, and frame the electorate's understanding of the issues of the day.

Another feature that distinguishes elections in the 1800s from contemporary ones is the fact that in that earlier period, Congress received more media coverage than the presidency, and most Americans expected Congress to take the lead on major policy issues. The country continued to expand—by 1876, the number of states, thirty-eight, was nearly three times what it had been when the Constitution was ratified—and this expansion raised complicated issues that sparked the imagination and excited the interests of many citizens. The range of issues that needed to be addressed included how to accommodate the increasing number of immigrants, how to deal with Native Americans, and how to bind this large, empire-sized country with a transportation system of roads, canals, and railroads. Of significant importance prior to the Civil War was the issue of slavery; as each new territory applied for statehood, Congress had to address whether the new state would be a free state or a slave state.

On most of these issues facing the nation, Congress took center stage. One measure of that is the amount of newspaper space devoted to congressional affairs. "Congress," as one historian noted, "got the lion's share of column inches. Newspapers routinely printed lengthy summaries of congressional debates as well as congressional commentary. Popular culture kept pace. By the 1850s there was a virtual school of Congress-bashing, in . . . plays, cartoons, even mock epic-poetry. All of these efforts were filled with inside jokes grounded on the assumption that the reading public was remarkably knowledgeable about the day-to-day happenings in Congress."[5]

Campaigns and election days throughout much of the nineteenth century were often raucous and tumultuous. Newspapers were an essential electioneering tool. They included emotional and often sensational language geared toward capturing people's attention and motivating them to vote for the party with which they were aligned. Party activists did not shy away from using newspapers to hurl insults and accusations against their partisan opponents. An example of this sort of campaign discourse occurred in the 1820s when President John Quincy Adams and Secretary of State Henry Clay were accused by some of Andrew Jackson's supporters of having stolen the 1824 election. The current concern in some quarters that President Trump had an inappropriate relationship with Vladimir Putin, the leader of Russia, is not the first time that a president has been accused of such a thing. The same Democrats who accused President Adams of election theft also claimed that he had secured prostitutes for the Russian czar. Adams's supporters in turn accused Jackson of being an adulterer and a murderer, and some called his mother a prostitute who had attended to British soldiers.[6]

Election days reflected a similar passion. They were filled with energy, intensity, and even a festive, holiday-like spirit. Political parties organized bands, torchlight parades, and door-to-door contacts to get voters to the polls. Politicians hired skilled speakers to entertain the large crowds that gathered to vote, and they provided plenty of food and drink—often alcoholic beverages—to entice their supporters to show up and vote.

Another feature of congressional elections added to the spirited partisanship of the era's election-day activities. Unlike today, state governments did not produce the ballots that citizens used to cast their votes. Instead, each party made its own unique ballot. Ballots often had a distinctive color, so, for instance, in some elections, Democrats' ballots might have been bright blue while Republicans' ballots might have been bright red. Sometimes these partisan-created ballots only listed candidates from their party on the ticket, so it was unusually difficult for someone showing up with a party-created ballot to vote for anyone other than that party's candidates. Split-ticket voting—selecting candidates from different parties for different political offices—is often easy to do today but could not be so readily accomplished in the nation's first one hundred years of existence. In addition, the parties often had their own officials watching polling places, so if they spotted the color of the ballot a potential voter was carrying as they made their way to vote, they knew which party that voter was likely to support. Coming on the heels of months of impassioned newspaper articles and campaign activities, and surrounded by large crowds of boisterous, alcohol-fueled fellow partisans, party officials sometimes urged fellow partisans to block someone from voting if they approached the polls with another party's ballot in hand. Indeed, by one count, eighty-nine Americans were killed at the polls during election day fights in the mid-1800s.[7]

Such rollicking and partisan-charged congressional elections frequently brought to the Capitol lawmakers who were less than distinguished, which, in turn, yielded high levels of turnover in office. As discussed earlier, most lawmakers did not view service on the Hill as a career until the closing decades of the nineteenth century. Moreover, many of these lawmakers were more than happy to use the same confrontational and freewheeling tactics in their legislative work that they enlisted in their election contests. In the House, members of the minority party, Democrats as well as Republicans, used parliamentary practices to bog things down and frustrate the majority. They called for points of order, demanded a reading of bills, asked that the roll be taken, and initiated other technical rules that temporarily prevented the House from taking any action. When those maneuvers failed, they simply refused to answer when their names were called at the beginning of a legislative day. This so-called disappearing quorum made it impossible for the House to finish much of its legislative business. Bills stayed in committees or were sidetracked on the floor. In 1885, for example, by one count, eleven thousand bills had died in committee without ever getting a floor vote when the Forty-Eighth Congress adjourned.[8]

INSTITUTIONAL CHANGE AND ELECTIONS: 1880s–1920s

Industrialization in the United States in the late nineteenth century brought new challenges and changes to congressional elections. Meanwhile, chamber leaders managed to get more control over a legislative process that had become unruly and unproductive. As Congress gained a greater capacity to act, its activities expanded, as did the role of the central government. Corporate leaders in the timber, oil, railroad, banking, and mining businesses, recognizing the growing role of the national government and eager to influence its decisions in ways that worked to their advantage, donated generously to party organizations. Industry's leaders wanted parties to recruit and put into office members who were sympathetic to their interests. They also used their financial clout to shape decisions of state legislators, who still selected U.S. senators at the time. Parties welcomed the assistance provided by corporate interests, for they needed the resources to run their campaigns, mobilize voters, and win elections.

Once in office, representatives and senators bowed to powerful party chamber leaders, who rewarded them with plum committee assignments and used their control over the levers of power to persuade rank-and-file members to vote the way that their party leaders wanted them to. Leaders, in turn, served the parties' corporate supporters, pressuring members to pass legislation those supporters wanted and blocking those they opposed. One veteran newspaper reporter, reminiscing in 1906 about how his job had changed, noted that "in the 1880s he had to know what almost every member of the House thought about a bill in order to predict its passage or defeat, requiring about 16 hours a day of hustling just to keep up." By the 1890s, he recalled, the easiest way to figure out a bill's fate was to talk with a handful of chamber leaders.[9]

Political parties' addiction to corporate election money was widespread. Investigations conducted shortly after the turn of the century revealed that "corporations and their chief officers had given somewhere between one- and three-quarters of the war chests of Republican and Democratic National committees since 1896." Corporations gained leverage over members in return for their contributions, and parties used this infusion of cash to run campaigns and even buy votes. Few regulations existed to curb such activity.[10]

Around the turn of the century, however, the scale of this corruption became so great as to become a source of alarm to many Americans. It also drew the attention of a new generation of journalists not aligned with political parties. Those journalists conducted hard-hitting investigations that resulted in explosive stories featuring congressional scandals. These scandals exposed the power of the wealthy and began to tarnish Congress's reputation. It became common, for instance, to refer to the Senate as "the millionaires club."

This steady media parade of dramatic accounts of congressional corruption helped to create a new set of activists and political reformers known as the "progressives," who pushed for reforms to break wealthy industrialists' stranglehold over political parties. One of the progressives' first successes was the adoption of primary elections. A primary election is an election in which citizens vote to determine the nominee who will run under their party's banner in the general election. By 1910, progressives convinced more than half the states to use primary elections to select a party's Senate candidate.[11] This reform, which takes power away from the party elite and gives it to the people, took root and eventually spread to include primaries to select party House and Senate candidates as well as presidential candidates.

Another one of the progressives' reforms was the adoption of the "Australian ballot," a nonpartisan ballot that stripped parties of their ability to create and distribute their own party-centered ballots. The Australian ballot gave citizens more privacy when they voted. It also made it easier for voters to split their ticket or support candidates from different parties for different offices.

Finally, the reformers managed to secure the adoption of two important constitutional amendments that directly affected elections. The first was the Seventeenth Amendment, which called for direct election of senators. The second was the Nineteenth Amendment, which was ratified in 1920. This amendment gave women the right to vote in all elections. Combined, these reforms dramatically expanded the number of Americans who had a direct say in choosing who represented them in Congress and further diminished the parties' control over congressional elections.

INSTITUTIONAL CHANGE AND ELECTIONS: 1920s–1970s

As a result of these developments, congressional campaigns changed. Initially, this was most noticeable in senatorial contests. Whereas in the past Senate candidates needed to be able to negotiate successfully with state party leaders behind closed doors to win the endorsement of their state legislature, they now had to appeal directly to the people and ask for their votes. This required a different kind of personality and skill set. Senators elected before the adoption of the Seventeenth Amendment did not often have to appear before crowds of voters, and when they did, the venues were more formal and staged.

After 1920, Senate candidates ran campaigns that more closely resembled those of their House colleagues. Like the House, candidates for the Senate attended informal gatherings and potluck dinners in church halls, town squares, and public parks to make their election appeals to the voters. They dropped all pretenses and frequently referred to themselves with shortened versions of their first names like Ed, Bill, or Joe. After making a speech, a Senate candidate would walk up to people, shake their hands, clap them on the shoulder, and make small talk. Just like House candidates, prospective senators needed to present themselves in ways that the public found pleasing and persuasive to create an image that resonated with ordinary Americans. Many of the sitting senators who lacked these sorts of skills or who were uncomfortable making these broad public appeals either retired or lost their seats.

Just as senators changed their campaign behavior, political parties also adjusted to the new political realities brought about by the reforms. By 1919, both parties created campaign committees designed to help their senatorial candidates win office, supplying them with advice, prepared speeches, and some financial support. Political parties also organized communication campaigns that portrayed their candidates favorably in newspapers and magazines, contacted voters with targeted, direct mailings, and by the late 1920s took advantage of the publicity opportunities provided by the new medium of radio.

But while they continued to play some role in congressional campaigns, party support was no longer as essential as it had been in the late 1800s and early 1900s. In that earlier time, parties spent a great deal of time recruiting candidates and then helping them get elected to office. With the introduction of primaries as well as the direct election of senators, candidates more often self-selected to run for Congress rather than wait to be asked to do so by a political party. Many candidates began to gather on their own the resources they needed to mount campaigns. As a result, parties lost some control over the candidates they would field in the general election. Campaigns thus became a more shared activity between parties and candidates.

THE PROFESSIONALIZATION OF CONGRESS

As members of Congress began to exercise more control over their own campaigns, other changes were underway that induced many representatives and senators to want to stay in office longer than their predecessors in the late 1800s. As noted in chapter 2, in the 1930s and 1940s the national government extended its policy reach with the New Deal's response to the Great Depression. Since Congress was now playing a major role in the day-to-day lives of many Americans, lawmakers started to see congressional service as a career instead of a temporary job they could use to jump-start a business or a legal practice. Members quickly realized they could use certain strategies and the benefits of their office to compensate for the declining role played by parties. To increase their chances for electoral success, congressional incumbents in these years reshaped their campaigns and focused more on local concerns than national issues. They also used the perks of their office to curry favor with their constituents.

Incumbents started to concentrate on helping to smooth the relationship that their constituents had with government agencies. They could, for instance, contact the Social Security Administration to see why a constituent's Social Security check had not arrived or provide the paperwork needed for a local construction firm to apply for a government contract. Members also worked to bring special projects that provided governmental funds—and thus jobs—back to their districts or states. Examples of these projects, sometimes called "pork," include things such as a new post office or a bridge or a military base. Members also provided themselves with more office staff to help them with this constituency-oriented work. And since they were already in power and had influence over policy decisions, incumbents found it much easier than their challengers to raise money from interest groups and others who wanted access to the corridors of power. Representatives and senators often received favorable local media coverage for these activities, which they hoped voters would remember at the next election. The franking privilege—the ability members have to send mail to their constituents without having to pay for postage—was another advantage they enjoyed over those who ran against them. Legislators were careful to take credit for these kinds of accomplishments in these mailings, which helped convince voters that they were doing a good job.

All of these factors gave incumbents a real advantage over those who ran against them, and partly as a result of this, it became increasingly easier for members to spend a long time in office. The successful reelection of incumbents continues to this day. Reelection rates for House members have generally hovered around 80–90 percent for the last half century, and the same has been true for incumbent senators in all but a handful of election years. Many representatives also find themselves holding "safe seats," which means that they regularly get more than 55 percent of the vote in an election. Some are so safe that they rarely attract anything more than a token opponent.

When they addressed more controversial and more national public policy matters, it was not uncommon for congressional members in the middle decades of the twentieth century to emphasize that they did not necessarily agree with their parties' positions on such issues. Members often declared that they were somewhat independent from their party's program, even when their party was in the majority or when it controlled the White House.

Advice that Tip O'Neill often gave his Democratic colleagues captures the spirit of this style of representation. O'Neill was a towering figure in congressional politics in this era. First elected to the House in 1953, he served as Speaker from 1977 to 1987 and is the only Speaker in the history of the House to serve for five complete consecutive Congresses. He regularly reminded his fellow legislators that "all politics is local." What he meant is that lawmakers needed to take care of their constituents, and they needed to be able to explain their votes to the folks back home in a way that they would find persuasive.

Successful congressional candidates thus developed what political scientist Richard Fenno called a "home style." In part, this involved strategically adjusting how they presented their party's policy positions to the citizens who voted them into office.[12] This style of representation, where individual legislators had lots of leeway to distance themselves from the policy positions of their parties, was possible in part because the parties were not ideologically cohesive. As noted in other chapters, the Republicans and Democrats each had liberal and conservative wings in these years, which created what might be thought of as a kind of political "space" within which individual representatives and senators could maneuver.

INSTITUTIONAL CHANGE AND ELECTIONS: 1980–2020

The political landscape was on the cusp of a major change just as Tip O'Neill was winding up his tenure as Speaker. By then, the parties were in the latter stages of sorting themselves out ideologically. By the early 1990s, most liberal voters identified as Democrats, while most conservatives identified as Republicans. Polling data from the American National Election Study (ANES) that track the trends in the average scores of Democratic and Republican Senate voters over several decades illustrate this change. In 1972, 30 percent of the Democrats who voted in a Senate election identified themselves as conservative. By 2008, that had fallen to 19 percent. Republican voters mirrored this change. While 43 percent of self-described conservative voters in a Senate election supported Republican candidates in 1972, 72 percent of them did so in 2008.[13]

The ideological polarization of the parties had a profound impact on congressional campaigns and on the style of representation that was rewarded with victory on election day. Most contemporary members of Congress seeking reelection stress their allegiance to the policy positions taken by their national parties. Rather than orient their campaigns around local themes, they are more likely to prominently proclaim that they will faithfully support the goals that their parties have identified. One way to explain this transformation of congressional campaign behavior is to note that many voters today view these legislative contests as an affirmation of their own ideological priorities and as local expressions of their support of their parties' national agenda. Speaker O'Neill's observation that all politics is local has now been turned on its head. The separation of American liberals and conservatives into opposing parties has had the effect of nationalizing congressional campaigns.

This ideological distribution of voters impacts congressional elections in yet another way. For the Senate, fewer states are truly competitive today, since in many states a majority of their citizens are either reliably conservative or reliably liberal. This puts those who challenge Senate incumbents at a real disadvantage. This dynamic is even more pronounced for representatives. Of the 435 House members, only about 15–20 percent of them come from districts that are competitive. One explanation for this is that House districts are gerrymandered, which means that state legislatures controlled by one party or the other draw House district boundaries in ways that make sure their party will almost always win the general elections there. The term *gerrymander* was coined by a politician who commented on a Massachusetts district that was approved by Governor Elbridge Gerry, a leading political figure of the republic's founding generation. As the story goes, the district, which was oddly shaped, looked like a salamander, prompting someone to quip that it was really a "Gerrymander."

As the number of safe House seats has grown, so, too, has the importance of primary elections. Since the outcome of the November general election is almost a foregone conclusion in safe districts, the real question is who will win the primary election. Most eligible voters do not turn out for primary elections, and those that do tend to be the most ideologically extreme. Republicans who vote in primary elections tend to be not only more conservative than most Americans but also more conservative than most Republicans. The same is true on the Democratic side, where primary voters tend to be more liberal than even most Democrats. To survive these primary battles, members need to adopt a certain style of representation. They must promise to support the party's agenda, work to enact it if elected, and resist efforts to compromise with the other party. As this dynamic took hold and made its way into congressional campaigns in the 1990s and beyond, it reinforced the ideological polarization it reflected.

The few moderate members left in both parties find it increasingly difficult to hold onto their legislative seats, and they tend to toe the party line when it comes to issues that the party considers especially critical. Recent experiences of some moderate senators illustrate the difficult terrain they must negotiate during elections in these more highly charged partisan times. Take the case of Republican Arlen Specter, a political centrist who was elected to a Pennsylvania Senate seat in 1980 and served there for thirty years. Confronted with facing a strong primary challenge from a conservative Republican in 2009, he decided to switch parties and run as a Democrat. He was defeated. Republican Lincoln Chafee, a moderate senator from Rhode Island who also tried to straddle the differences between the parties, managed to overcome a difficult conservative primary challenge in 2006 but was so weakened by that fight that he went on to lose in the general election.

The fate of two other Senate moderates in recent times, both extraordinarily accomplished, help demonstrate how deeply polarized contemporary congressional elections have become and how difficult it is for moderate politicians to stray from their party. Joseph Lieberman, a longtime Connecticut Democrat elected to the Senate in 1988, was reelected three times. He was also chosen to be his party's vice presidential candidate in the 2000 general election. Six years later, perceived as out of step with his party for his support of the Iraq War, Senator Lieberman was defeated in a primary election. Though he ran as an independent in that fall's general election and won, the party that had trusted him with their vice presidential nomination at the turn of the century rebuffed him as a senatorial candidate only six years later.

The arc of Indiana Republican Richard Lugar's career tells the same story. A two-term mayor of Indianapolis, he gave the keynote address at the 1972 Republican presidential nominating convention. Elected to the Senate in 1976, he went on to win five more Senate contests. He was so popular that in 2006 the Democrats chose not to field a candidate to run against him. Throughout his career, he was open to working across the aisle and on occasion even voted against his party. For instance, he supported President Barack Obama's nominees, Sonia Sotomayor and Elena Kagan, to fill vacancies on the Supreme Court. And after the breakup of the Soviet Union in 1989, he worked alongside Senator Sam Nunn, a Georgia Democrat, to put in place mechanisms to monitor that former superpower's nuclear arsenal so that it would not fall into the hands of terrorists or rogue states. In early 2012, facing a stiff primary challenge from a conservative Republican, Lugar's office put out a press release denying that President Obama called him for advice. In the earlier era when Lugar first entered the Senate, a call from the president of another party would have been a source of pride and a sign of influence. But not in the political environment of the 2010s, when even the hint of bipartisanship invited the prospect of a primary challenge that could bring an abrupt end to a political career. Senator Lugar lost his 2012 Republican primary election to an opponent who, when asked what his idea of bipartisanship was, said that his idea of bipartisanship was that the Democrats do what the Republicans want them to do. This sort of electoral outcome reinforces partisanship on the Hill, since few are willing to risk ending their career in a bruising primary election.

CONCLUSION

Tracing the history of congressional elections reveals how they simultaneously shape, and are shaped by, the larger political system of which they are a part. In some eras, elections have produced congressional members who are fiercely independent actors who resist being led by chamber leaders, while in other times, elections have attracted members who are quite willing to do the bidding of their parties. Some electoral cycles have been dominated by candidates interested in compromising and finding common ground with their partisan opponents, while other cycles have punished those with that inclination. Electoral success has, at times, depended on the ability of candidates to negotiate quietly with political elites behind closed doors; at other times, it has rewarded those candidates able to communicate a highly partisan message persuasively in an open public forum. In this sense, congressional elections are a kind of barometer that measure and reflect the forces that drive the American political system.

NOTES

1. Philip Bump, "At Least 21 Members Are Registered to Vote Outside of Their Districts," *Washington Post*, June 20, 2017, https://www.washingtonpost.com /news/politics/wp/2017/04/21/at-least-20-members-of-the-house-are-registered -to-vote-outside-their-districts.

2. James Madison, *Federalist Paper No. 52*, in *The Founders' Constitution*, eds. Philip B. Kurland and Ralph Lerner, 5 vols. (Indianapolis, IN: Liberty Fund, 2001), http://press-pubs.uchicago.edu/founders/documents/a1_2_1s14.html.

3. Richard Fenno, "If, as Ralph Nader Says, Congress Is 'the Broken Branch,' How Come We Love Our Congressmen So Much?," paper prepared for delivery at a conference on the role of Congress, sponsored by Time Inc. at the Harvard Club, Boston, MA, December 12, 1972, reprinted in *American Government: Readings and Cases*, 14th ed., ed. Peter Woll (New York: Longman, 2001), 384–91.

4. See Peveril Squire, *The Evolution of American Legislatures: Colonies, Territories, and States, 1619–2009* (Ann Arbor: University of Michigan Press, 2014).

5. Joanne B. Freeman, *The Field of Blood: Violence in Congress and the Road to Civil War* (New York: Farrar, Straus and Giroux, 2018), 27.

6. Robert W. Remini, *The House: The History of the House of Representatives* (New York: HarperCollins, 2007), 117.

7. Jill Lepore, "Rocks, Papers, Scissors: How We Used to Vote," *New Yorker*, October 6, 2008, https://www.newyorker.com/magazine/2008/10/13/rock-paper-scissors.

8. Remini, *The House*, 243.

9. Peter Swenson, "The Influence of Recruitment on The Structure of Power in the U.S. House, 1870–1940," *Legislative Studies Quarterly* VII, no. 1 (February 1982): 11–12.

10. Eric Rauchway, "The Transformation of the Congressional Experience," in *The American Congress: The Building of Democracy*, ed. Julian E. Zelizer (New York: Houghton Mifflin, 2004), 323.

11. Neil MacNeil and Richard Baker, *The American Senate: An Insider's History* (New York: Oxford University Press, 2013), 21.

12. See Richard Fenno, *Home Style: House Members in Their Districts* (New York: Pearson, 2003).

13. Alan Abramowitz, "U.S. Senate Elections in a Polarized Era," in *The U.S. Senate: From Deliberation to Dysfunction*, ed. Burdett A. Loomis (Washington, DC: CQ Press, 2012), 33.

4

Congressional Committees

Congressional committees play a key role in congressional politics. Sometimes called "little legislatures" or Congress's "workshops," committees and their subcommittees are where representatives and senators do much of their legislative work.[1] It is in committee and subcommittee meetings that members review bills and hold hearings to gather information from executive branch officials, lobbyists, academics, and others who have expertise on public problems and policy issues. It is there that members of Congress deliberate and bargain with one another as they revise or mark up bills. And it is in those little legislatures or workshops that decisions are made on whether to send bills forward to the full House or full Senate or to let them languish and die. Given the careful attention committee members often give to the bills they report out, their Capitol Hill colleagues are usually inclined to support their recommendations. This means that for many bills, the critical decision as to whether they become law is effectively made by committees. As Woodrow Wilson once put it, "Congress in session is Congress on public exhibition, whilst Congress in its committee rooms is Congress at work."[2]

This chapter explains the different types of committees Congress uses, reviews their different activities, and discusses how members get assigned to them. It also explores how committee behavior and committee changes over time are impacted by congressional-executive relationships, by political parties, and by the internal jockeying for power between chamber leaders, committee chairs, and regular rank-and-file members. Understanding

51

why committees exist, why they act the way that they do, and why that behavior changes over time helps us see that Congress is, simultaneously, a distinctive political body and part of a larger, interrelated political order.

COMMITTEE TYPES

Article I of the Constitution says a lot about Congress and its powers but nothing about committees. Yet committees have always been important to the institution. Initially, each chamber reviewed legislation through its Committee of the Whole, which is a parliamentary device that includes all members in the chamber. Once a chamber's Committee of the Whole reached a general consensus on a proposed measure, it appointed a select or temporary committee to translate that consensus into legislative language by writing a bill. When a select committee completed its work, it sent its bill back to the full chamber and was dissolved. The entire membership of each chamber, once again operating as a Committee of the Whole, would take up the select committee's draft of the bill, debate it, possibly amend it, and then vote on it.

Relying on select committees to write legislation and then having the Committee of the Whole assess every bill's sections proved to be cumbersome. Because each chamber's entire membership debated, amended, and voted on only one measure at a time, Congress got bogged down in its work. And since every member reviewed each proposal, lawmakers could not gain the expertise they needed to respond quickly and effectively to the domestic and international challenges that the new nation confronted.

Congress also encountered additional challenges as the size of the House and Senate expanded in response to the admission of new states into the Union. In 1789, the House had 65 members. After the 1790 census, it had 106 members. Its numbers increased to 142 in 1800, to 186 in 1810, and then to 213 in 1820.[3] In less than a half century, the number of House members more than tripled in size. That was too large a body to have the entire membership draft, amend, and vote on every bill.

To rectify this unwieldy legislative process, first the House and then the Senate began to create permanent standing committees. Unlike select committees, which are dissolved after they finish their work, standing committees are embodied in the two chambers' rules and continue from one congressional session to the next. This brings greater order and predictability to congressional work. And because standing committees are charged with reviewing and making recommendations on specific types of policy issues, their members are given the chance to become knowledgeable on matters sent to their committee. The names of these committees often indicate the type of proposals that come their way. Early standing committees, for example, included the House Committee on Elections, established in 1790, and the House Interstate and Foreign Commerce Committee, which was created in 1795.

From 1809 through 1825, the number of House standing committees increased from 10 to 28, while the number of select committees fell from 350 to less than 70. That changing ratio of standing House committees to select House committees illustrates that the reliance on the Committee of the Whole and select committees had given way to one dominated by standing committees. In the early 1820s, House standing committees gained the power to bypass the Committee of the Whole and report bills directly to the floor. They could also effectively kill a bill by refusing to report it out of committee.

The Senate lagged behind the House in creating standing committees. But the War of 1812 and the need to oversee the executive branch more systematically changed that. During that conflict, any senator could introduce a bill directly just by giving notice. Although the then-dominant Democratic-Republican Party held 82 percent of the Senate seats, dissident senators used that strategy to distract and derail the Senate majority from overseeing the administration's war efforts. Experiences like that moved the Senate to extend the life of its select committees by giving them new assignments instead of disbanding them after they completed their work. As a result, many select committees started to look and act a bit like standing committees. In 1816, the Senate took the formal step of converting eleven such select committees into permanent ones. By the mid-1820s, standing committees were firmly in place and at the center of the Congress's activities.[4]

Today the House has twenty standing committees, and the Senate has seventeen. Changes in their number, jurisdiction, and responsibilities can only be done by changing congressional rules. But this is not easy to do, since members have vested interests in the committees on which they serve. As a result of their work in committees, members have ongoing relationships with other political actors, including interest groups and officials in the executive branch. These relationships are difficult to disturb, resulting in committee members who are reluctant to accept change.

While standing committees conduct Congress's routine business, both chambers periodically still create select committees to address specific issues, problems, or events. Select committees, sometimes called special committees, have been created in response to any pressing issue that catches the public's attention, or to study an issue that cannot be adequately addressed by standing committees. Occasionally, a select committee can be quite influential.

For instance, in 1973, the Senate created a Select Committee to Investigate Presidential Campaign Activities as a response to a scandal that implicated members of President Richard Nixon's administration. Known as the Watergate scandal, that incident involved an illegal break-in to the campaign office of President Nixon's 1972 presidential opponent, Senator George McGovern, a Democrat from South Dakota. Watergate centered on efforts by the president and his aides to cover up the White House's involvement in the break-in. Convened to investigate this scandal, that select committee's meetings received extensive media coverage.

A highlight of its work was the question posed by one of its Republican members, Tennessee senator Howard Baker: "What did the president know, and when did he know it?" That question became one of the most famous ever asked in the Senate, and it has been asked in many subsequent investigations into possible presidential misconduct.[5] That committee's hearings made it clear that President Nixon was losing the support of even Republican senators, and most observers think that its work contributed to the president's decision to resign. More recently, in 2020, the House's Permanent Select Committee on Intelligence played a leading role in the House's first impeachment proceeding against President Donald Trump.

In addition to standing and select committees, two other committee types bear mentioning: the joint committee and the conference committee. Joint committees are composed of lawmakers from both houses. They are not directly involved in Congress's legislative activities; instead, they either perform housekeeping tasks or conduct periodic studies on matters with which the House and Senate regularly deal. For instance, the current Joint Committee on Printing oversees the activities of the Government Publishing Office, while the Joint Committee on Taxation provides members with reports on tax policy.

The other type of committee, the conference committee, also includes members from both chambers. Conference committees are temporary bodies created to iron out differences in bills that pass both the House and the Senate but are not in identical form. Conference committees aim to draft a report that marks a compromise between the two versions. When finished, a conference committee's report goes back to the House and Senate, where each chamber holds a floor vote and the committee's report is either accepted or rejected. Since those are the only two options available to members, in practice this means that conference committees often have the last say in shaping a law's details.

COMMITTEES AND INSTITUTIONAL POWER

The move to replace select committees with standing committees during the 1820s decentralized power within Congress. Select committees, after all, were responsive to the House and Senate majorities that created them. Chamber majorities decided who sat on select committees, defined their missions, and, if they were unhappy with their progress, could disband them at a moment's notice and create a new one. Also, when acting as a Committee of the Whole, if a chamber's majority wanted to make a final up or down vote on a bill without sending it to a committee, they could do so. There was no tradition or rule stipulating that floor votes should occur only after a committee reviewed bills and made its recommendations to the full body. The relatively permanent status of standing committees, combined with their authority to refuse to bring bills up for floor votes, gave them an autonomy within the chambers that select committees never enjoyed. Though standing committees' ability to resist their chambers' majorities has changed over the years, they have always played an important role in shaping House and Senate actions.

This gives rise to a question: Why would the House and Senate agree to create a committee system that on occasion is able to frustrate, and sometimes even defeat, what a majority wants? Part of the answer to that question lies in the congressional workload. As the country's population grew and its territorial reach expanded with the introduction of new states, the sheer number of issues that the legislature had to deal with increased tremendously. By one estimate, the House in the first Congress took up a total of 149 bills. From 1947 to 2014, the fewest number of bills introduced into the House in any one session was 3,809. In 2019, the House and Senate, combined, entertained 10,911 measures.[6]

As the volume of congressional legislation increased over time, so did the complexity of the policy problems its members confronted. Standing committees are an organizational response to these institutional challenges. In its first years, the United States negotiated a complicated relationship with England, France, and Spain in order to keep those powers from infringing on American rights and interests. The United States also had to manage a decades-long, troubled relationship with Native Americans who already held the land and resources desired by the expanding nation. Later, as industrialization took hold in the late 1800s and early 1900s, Congress needed to acquaint itself with novel and complex financial, banking, and investment arrangements; new modes of transportation, such as railroads and automobiles; and new communications technologies, such as the telegraph and the telephone. All of these changes upended traditional social relations and governmental arrangements and linked the country together in new ways just as it was taking on a new and leading role on the world stage.

Today a few of the issues that the contemporary Congress has to deal with include climate change, nuclear and chemical weapons, genetic engineering, a rapidly evolving digital economy, and a highly integrated global economy. These issues highlight the vast kinds of technical expertise that today's Congress must master in its work. Standing committees help Congress develop the institutional intelligence required to respond to such sweeping socioeconomic transformations. House and Senate majorities have been willing to cede some power to committees because it helps them manage workloads and gain policy expertise. The hope is that committee members will invest time and energy learning about issues their committee addresses.

To encourage members to further narrow their focus and add to the depth of their expertise, most committees have several subcommittees. Committees and their subcommittees thus enable lawmakers to engage those political actors who make a living dealing with those issues on an equal footing—so the legislature is not at a disadvantage when it deals with executive branch officials, presidential aides, and special interests' private lobbyists. As a result of their specialization, committee members can amass important knowledge they can share with other lawmakers when the full chambers debate and vote on a bill reported from the committee. In return, committee members gain leverage and power within their chambers. For example, other lawmakers will usually defer to committee members on the measures they report to their full chambers, frequently following the committee's recommendations when they debate and vote on the House and Senate floors. Standing committees can also significantly slow down bills or refuse to report them to the floor. These practices signal to other political actors just how much power standing-committee members wield on policies that fall within their domain, and they encourage not only other members of Congress but also executive branch officials and interest groups to treat seriously committee members' policy preferences. So the privileged place that standing committees usually hold in the legislative process simultaneously serves the institutional needs of the entire legislature as well as the personal goals of its individual members.

CONGRESSIONAL COMMITTEES AND EXECUTIVE OVERSIGHT

Another important congressional function that both chambers entrust to their committees is executive oversight. The power to oversee executive branch activity and to investigate executive branch behavior is inextricably intertwined with Congress's legislative responsibilities. To make sensible laws, Congress needs information, some of which is in the hands of the president, presidential aides, advisers, and the more permanent members of the executive branch or the bureaucracy. Committees are the primary tool Congress relies on to see to it that the president is "faithfully executing" laws it passes. This includes making sure that appropriated money is being used by the executive branch for the purposes Congress intended. Congress also engages in oversight to assess whether conditions have changed in ways that require adjustments in the administration's authority or in existing policies. Finally, Congress needs to investigate whenever there is credible evidence that executive officials, including the president and high-ranking members of the administration, may have mishandled the public's business.

Presidents and members of the administration do not always appreciate oversight and the investigations it generates. This is especially true under conditions of divided government, when one party controls the White House and another party controls the Congress. Yet while that sort of party divide can intensify the conflict that oversight engenders, the more enduring source of interbranch dissension here is the Constitution's decision to simultaneously separate these two institutions and give them overlapping authority. The friction this predictably creates between the Congress and the White House exists even when both are in the hands of the same party. Executive officials regularly protest that these congressional actions are unfair attacks masquerading as constitutionally required duties and that they amount to an unconstitutional attempt by the legislature to encroach on presidential powers. One way this tension between the two branches expresses itself is when a congressional committee summons an executive official either to meet with and perhaps testify in front of a committee hearing or to turn over documents in the executive branch's possession. On occasion, presidents and executive branch officials turn to the courts and ask the judiciary to support their refusal to cooperate with these legislative inquiries.

The first congressional investigation of executive branch behavior was authorized on March 27, 1792, when the House created a committee to investigate "the Battle of the Wabash." At that battle, American forces led by Major General Arthur St. Clair were defeated by Native American warriors near the present site of Fort Recovery, Ohio. Little Turtle, a Sagamore, or leader of the Wabash people, coordinated a series of surprise attacks and imaginative battlefield maneuvers that led to a staggering defeat of the Americans. "The totality of the Indian victory," as one account put it, "was unprecedented: 657 U.S. soldiers dead and 271 wounded, not counting an unknown number of fatalities among the camp followers. It was a devastating defeat for American arms. It would be the greatest win ever for an Indian army fighting against a U.S. force, far surpassing the better-known victory over George Armstrong Custer's Seventh Cavalry 85 years later."[7]

After the House authorized a special committee to ask for all "such persons, papers, and records as may be necessary to assist their inquiries," President George Washington asked members of his cabinet for their opinions as to whether he should comply. All of them—Secretary of Treasury Alexander Hamilton, Secretary of State Thomas Jefferson, Secretary of War Henry Knox, and Attorney General Edmund Randolph—agreed that the House had the right to ask for this information and that the president should withhold only that evidence "the disclosure of which would harm the public." Washington followed their advice.

The House committee's initial finding was that contract fraud was responsible for the defeat. Secretary Knox and his quartermaster were blamed for outfitting the military with shoddy supplies. Knox denied the findings, claiming that the investigation was one sided, while asserting that House members had leaked parts of their work to the press to turn public opinion against him. After receiving Knox's rebuttal of over one hundred pages and piles of affidavits from the quartermaster as part of a blizzard of claims and counterclaims, the committee softened its conclusions but still largely laid the blame at Knox's feet.[8]

The claims and counterclaims of this initial congressional investigation are recurring features of congressional-presidential relations. More than a half century after the Knox affair, here's how one member of Congress described a similar congressional investigation of possible executive branch malfeasance: "We all know that when those committees had gorged themselves with accusations against men, made by persons of no character and standing in the community, they were permitted to ooze out to newspaper correspondents, thus establishing a sort of competition with each other on the subject of the slander of men and measures."[9] After his election in 2016, President Trump echoed similar sentiments, regularly complaining that congressional committees reviewing his administration's affairs conspired with reporters by releasing partial and incomplete information to undermine his presidency. One such incident centered on whether President Trump and some of his associates within the administration and outside of it had pressured the Ukrainian government to investigate former vice president Joseph Biden to see if they could uncover damaging information about him. The president vigorously denied that he had any hand in that kind of activity. However, several executive branch and White House officials with years of experience in American foreign policy stepped forward to say that, after participating in a July 25, 2019, phone call between President Trump and the president of the Ukraine, they were concerned that he was not only involved in these efforts but that he may have been directing them.

The larger point here for our purposes is to note that the sort of friction and acrimony generated by congressional oversight investigations of executive branch behavior is not simply, or even primarily, caused by the personalities and character of particular presidents, representatives, and senators. Presidents and their supporters are inclined to disparage the motives of those reviewing executive activities. Congress and their allies tend to suspect White House claims that the only reason presidents refuse to turn over evidence is to preserve the constitutional integrity of the office. While the details of how this interbranch relationship plays out differs from case to case, the larger pattern of this kind of institutional clash is remarkably similar. The constitutional scheme created by the framers and accepted by every subsequent generation of Americans is designed to produce this sort of institutional rivalry.

Not all presidents and their aides have been as cooperative in congressional investigations as Washington and his cabinet. Take the case of President Warren G. Harding's administration and the investigation into a scandal involving a member of his cabinet. When this scandal, known as the Teapot Dome scandal, came to light, many suspected that Attorney General Henry Daugherty was involved. A Senate committee investigating the scandal ordered his brother Mally, a bank president, to testify before it and share documents relevant to the investigation. When Mally refused, he was arrested for contempt, which he claimed in court was a power that the Congress did not possess. The case involving his contempt conviction went all the way to the Supreme Court. In its decision, *McGrain v. Daugherty* (1927), the Supreme Court upheld the Senate's action and ruled that Congress does have the power to compel witnesses to come before it and provide testimony.

The Supreme Court made a similar ruling a few years later. As a part of its investigation of possible corruption at the U.S. Post Office, the chairman of a special Senate committee created to look into the matter, Senator Hugo Black, a Democrat from Alabama, ordered an attorney named William MacCracken to turn over the papers of some of his clients. When MacCracken refused, the Senate ordered its sergeant at arms to arrest MacCracken and bring him to the Senate chamber. The Senate subsequently put him on trial, found him guilty, and sentenced him to ten days for contempt of Congress. MacCracken appealed his conviction. In 1935, the Supreme Court ruled unanimously that Congress did indeed have the power to compel witnesses to give testimony, provide papers, and arrest those who ignored such legitimate demands.

Some forty years later, during the 1973 Watergate investigations, President Nixon initially said that he would not permit any of his aides to testify before the special Senate committee appointed to investigate alleged violations of the law by his administration and members of his reelection campaign. The chairman of the committee, Senator Sam Ervin, a Democrat from North Carolina, cited the *MacCracken* decision and declared he would order the arrest of the president's aides and force them to come before his committee. After that announcement, President Nixon changed his mind and withdrew his order forbidding his assistants from cooperating with the Senate.[10]

More recently, President Trump, citing executive privilege and the need to keep some presidential communication secret, was successful in preventing many members of his White House staff and other executive branch officials from cooperating with the House's impeachment investigation and the Senate's subsequent trial on those charges. As this matter played out, a three-judge panel of the federal appeals court overruled a federal district court order and, in a 2–1 decision, said that the House Judiciary Committee lacked the authority to compel the president's White House counsel to appear before it and testify. Each judge wrote a separate opinion, and while two of them voted to overrule the lower court, all three opinions expressed different understandings of what kind of power the Constitution gives to Congress in these sorts of situations.[11]

Participants in these clashes between Congress and the presidency often have different ideas about where the powers of the two branches begin and end, and the way they behave in these instances may be motivated by partisanship or by a desire to escape punishment as well as by their understanding of constitutional provisions. Yet these conflicts are unavoidable, because the two branches share powers. Congressional oversight is therefore a natural and predictable outcome of the United States' constitutional architecture, and congressional committees are the primary vehicles that the House and Senate use to carry it out.

COMMITTEES AND POLITICAL AMBITIONS

Committees also help lawmakers realize their political goals. Representatives and senators want to be assigned to committees that address issues and policies their constituents care about, which can help them get reelected. Beyond that, some members have specific policy interests they want to advance. They might be interested in, say, gun control measures, environmental issues, or educational or tax policies. Such policy-oriented lawmakers prefer seats on committees that enable them to shape outcomes on those matters. Still another set of lawmakers are especially interested in acquiring power on the Hill. They want to be able to influence Congress's work. These members, as one song in the musical *Hamilton* puts it, want "to be in the room where it happens." These three goals—getting reelected, determining policy outcomes, and gaining institutional power—are not mutually exclusive, and members might be motivated by all three. But for many, especially at different stages in their career, one goal tends to predominate. And, as studies of Congress point out, committees can be useful vehicles for helping members realize their goals.[12]

For instance, members from rural districts or those with a particular interest in food policy might work to get a seat on their chamber's Agriculture

Committee. Legislators with a large concentration of educators among their constituents or who have a keen interest in education policy might try hard to get on either the House Education and Labor committee or the Senate Health, Education, Labor and Pensions committee. Some committees enable members to gain power and exercise influence within their chamber. This has been especially true in the House, where some committees like Appropriations, Rules, and Ways and Means are traditionally considered to be especially important to the legislature's work. Service on these committees can be time-consuming, and their work rarely attracts much public attention. Yet the decisions that they make touch on functions that are at the heart of congressional work.

COMMITTEE MEMBERSHIPS AND POWER

The way committee assignments are made has changed over time and reflects different power relationships on the Hill. As congressional parties became stronger and more organized in the latter part of the nineteenth century, their members recognized they could shape legislative outcomes by exerting leverage over committees. Congressional parties in both chambers did this by determining the leadership and composition of committees.

The majority party controls the congressional agenda through committee chairs. Though their power has waxed and waned over time, committee chairs are among the most influential members in Congress. They often set their committee's priorities, determine its agenda, schedule its hearings, exert considerable control over its staff, and lead debate and deliberation on legislation reported by their committee to the full chamber as well as manage negotiations on any of their committee's legislation that makes it to a conference committee. The majority party also shapes the partisan composition of committees and exerts influence over them by giving itself more seats, thus increasing the likelihood that its positions will prevail when committees act. The distribution of committee seats in the House and the Senate generally reflects the chamber's party ratio, thus ensuring the majority's control. If, for example, one party has 60 percent of the seats while another has 40 percent of them, then the majority party will have something close to 60 percent of the seats on all but a few committees. Some committees, like the House Rules Committee, overrepresent the majority to ensure that the party's position in that committee will almost always prevail.

While congressional parties use leverage over who gets assigned to various committees and who gets to lead them, the way they make those decisions has evolved and changed. Much of this is the result of the strength or cohesiveness of the parties at any point in time. Moreover, there are important differences between the House and the Senate in how they make these decisions. These tend to reflect the different values and traditions of the two chambers.

The partisan divisions that emerged after the Civil War and Reconstruction impacted the House by contributing to a strengthening of the Speaker's powers. Speakers acquired a free hand in making committee assignments, which they strategically used to achieve their partisan goals. This strategic use of power, however, was not entirely new. Henry Clay, who served as the Speaker of the House in the early years of the nineteenth century, had done so as well. The differences, though, were that Clay did not face strong, competitive congressional parties, and permanent committees were not established fixtures in the House.

By the late nineteenth century, things were different. Committees played a significant role in the House's work, and Speakers had the backing of strong parties to support their actions. Speakers used their leverage to punish members who opposed them by assigning them to committees that were undesirable and often unrelated to their constituents' interests. Speakers also named committee chairs and used that as leverage to influence outcomes as well. For example, Speakers enlisted those handpicked chairs to bottle up legislation introduced by members who deviated from the Speaker's party line. All of this made life difficult for rebellious members. Representatives who resisted the Speakers' leadership often ended up sitting on committees where they could do little good for their constituents and were unable to pass any meaningful legislation, all of which put their political careers in jeopardy.

House members grew increasingly unhappy with the centralization of so much power in the hands of so few. This discontent stemmed from policy disagreements as well as members' changing career patterns. Republicans were divided on how to respond to industrialization and the effects it had on society. Some, representing a more progressive wing of the party, pushed for more regulation of big business. The Speaker in the early 1900s, Representative Joseph Cannon, a conservative Republican from Illinois, tried to stymie those efforts. Although Cannon's predecessor, Thomas Brackett Reed, a Republican from Maine, had used his powers as Speaker to prevent a House minority from obstructing legislation that the House majority favored, Cannon used his leverage to block legislation he personally opposed. Cannon's actions put him at odds with his party's more progressive members.

At the same time that this policy divide was brewing among Republican representatives, legislators started viewing service on the Hill as a career. They did not want the resources necessary for a successful career, like work on an important committee, to depend on the Speaker's whims and desires. Thus, many progressive Republicans joined forces with the opposition to strip away many of the Speaker's powers, including the ability to appoint committee chairs. They also agreed that going forward, they would use the "seniority rule" to appoint chairs of committees. This meant that the majority party member who had the most seniority—the longest term of uninterrupted service on a committee—was automatically named the chair, and the most senior member in the minority became the ranking minority member.

Protocol was slightly different in the Senate. Because of its traditions and rules, individual senators had more leeway. As is still the case today, the Senate lacked a strong presiding officer, such as the Speaker, who could single-handedly control committee appointments. Instead, the Senate relied more on consensus in reaching decisions. By the middle of the nineteenth century, senators settled on using seniority to make assignments; however, that was not an ironclad rule. That only happened later, once more senators started seeking reelection and treating service in that chamber as a career. But the Senate did start to rely on seniority as a way to distribute committee chairmanships earlier than the House did.[13]

THE RISE OF COMMITTEE CHAIRS

With the "rule of seniority" firmly in place, committee chairs enjoyed a privileged status and gradually accumulated significant powers. Committee chairs controlled committee meetings and determined the fate of bills within their jurisdiction. Chairs determined whether their committees had subcommittees and who led them, and they themselves were often voting members on every one of their subcommittees. They also controlled other committee resources such as committee staff members, whose numbers Congress increased to help it deal with the dramatic expansion of its workload after World War II. Chairs also determined who would manage legislation reported from their committees when it reached the floor, if they did not do so themselves. Especially in the House, members knew that no matter what goal or set of goals motivated them—the desire to get reelected, to shape policy, or to wield power in Congress—they needed to follow their committee chairs' lead if they wanted to succeed.[14]

The seniority rule had unintended consequences for the Democratic Party, which held the majority in both the Senate and House of Representatives through many of the decades in the middle of the twentieth century. It gave southern Democrats disproportionate influence on the Hill. After the Civil War, Republicans had almost no standing in states that had formed the Confederacy. This meant that in the general election southern Democrats had only token opposition. Unless they retired, sought other offices, died, or were defeated in a primary election, they continued to get reelected and kept climbing the ladder of seniority. This gave southern Democrats an advantage in the committee seniority system. The enormous powers that committee chairs enjoyed thus frequently served southern policy preferences at the expense of their more northern and midwestern Democratic colleagues, who took more progressive stances on civil rights policies, social welfare programs and, somewhat later, on the war in Vietnam. Southern Democratic representatives' and senators' positions on these and other issues were not shared by a majority of their fellow Democrats, but given the array of powers they wielded as committee chairs, they were consistently able to slow down, dilute, and even defeat many of the policy proposals a majority in their party preferred.

PARTISANSHIP AND THE CHANGING SHAPE OF POWER

As noted in chapter 2, change started to unfold in the late 1960s and early 1970s as the more liberal Democrats gained control of their party and curbed committee chairs' powers. Another set of reforms pushed through by House Democrats at the same time enhanced the power of chamber leaders. Though not immediately felt, these changes shifted power to the Speaker. They gave the Speaker power to determine the composition of the key committees and to decide what bills would get a hearing by the full House. The effect of these reforms became more apparent in the 1980s and 1990s, when the parties became more internally cohesive and polarized. With their party more firmly united behind them, Democratic leaders such as the Speaker started using these newly acquired powers over committees to get the outcomes their membership wanted. The same held true with Republicans. When Republicans gained control of the House in the election of 1994 after being in the minority for forty years, their leaders followed suit.

Senate party leaders have less leverage in shaping committees than their House counterparts do. Recall that Senate rules and traditions give its members more leeway and leverage. Still, even in the Senate, contemporary leaders have gained greater influence as a result of party changes, thus strengthening their hand in making committee assignments.

Today's committee chairs, while still important, can no longer ignore policies their party colleagues campaigned on and promised to pass. Instead, leaders in both chambers actively intervene to put in place committee chairs who they believe can best advance their party's agenda, even if, as is especially the case in the House, they must bypass seniority. Leaders of the two chambers turn to members whom they believe have the energy, experience, and savvy necessary to advance the party's initiative inside the chamber and mount a public relations campaign on its behalf outside of it. Leaders also use these slots to reward members who help the congressional party raise money from special interests that can be distributed to its candidates in elections. At the same time, chamber leaders work more closely with chairs to advance their party's initiatives and at times even intervene to craft changes to bills after legislation leaves committees and is sent to the floor for debate and a vote. And in some circumstances, leaders even bypass committees entirely and work with selected legislators and staff members to write legislation on their own.

In the one hundred plus years since the 1910 revolt against congressional leaders (see chapter 2), power in the House and Senate has in some sense come full circle. While committees and their chairs are still important in the legislative process, leaders, backed by more cohesive and ideological parties, are once again the most influential actors on the Hill.

CONCLUSION

Congressional committees play an important role in helping Congress meet its constitutional responsibilities. Though not mentioned in the Constitution, committees enable the institution to manage its legislative work and carry out its oversight responsibilities. Yet while they have long provided these services, the precise way they have done so has evolved over time. They have been shaped by changes on the larger political landscape, by Congress's relations with the executive branch, and by the motives and goals of the individuals who serve in the institution, including both leaders and rank-and-file members. Committees play a key role in helping Congress simultaneously respond to and shape the dynamic, sprawling enterprise that is the American experiment with democracy.

NOTES

1. George Goodwin Jr., *The Little Legislatures: Committees of Congress* (Amherst: University of Massachusetts Press, 1970); Colton C. Campbell and Roger H. Davidson, "U.S. Congressional Committees: Changing Legislative Workshops," *Journal of Legislative Studies* 4, no. 1 (1998): 124–42. For an overview of congressional committees, see Christopher J. Deering and Steven S. Smith, *Committees in Congress* (Washington, DC: CQ Press, 1997). A classic study on committees in the House is found in Richard Fenno, *Congressmen in Committees* (Boston: Little, Brown, 1973). For general treatment on the role of committees in Congress, see Benjamin Ginsberg and Kathryn Wagner Hill, *Congress: The First Branch* (New Haven, CT: Yale University Press, 2019); E. Scott Adler, Jeffery A. Jenkins, and Charles R. Shipan, *The United States Congress* (New York: W. W.

Norton, 2019), chap. 7; Donald Ritchie, *The U.S. Congress: A Very Short Introduction* (New York: Oxford University Press, 2016); and Roger Davidson, Walter J. Oleszek, Frances E. Lee, and Eric Shickler, *Congress and Its Members* (Thousand Oaks, CA: CQ Press, 2018).

2. Woodrow Wilson, *Congressional Government: A Study in American Politics* (Boston: Houghton Mifflin,1885; republished Baltimore, MD: Johns Hopkins University Press, 1981), 69.

3. Burdett A. Loomis, *The Contemporary Congress* (New York: St. Martin's Press, 1996), 16; Stephen Goode, *The New Congress* (New York: Julian Messner 1980), 63.

4. Goode, *The New Congress*, 68; U.S. Senate, "Senate Creates Permanent Committees," July 1, 2020, https://www.senate.gov/artandhistory/history/minute /Senate_Creates_Permanent_Committees.htm; and Donald R. Hickey, "The War of 1812," in *The American Congress*, ed. Julian E. Zelizer (New York: Houghton Mifflin, 2004), 95–96.

5. Appearing on Joe Scarborough's MSNBC show, *Morning Joe*, House Speaker Nancy Pelosi was asked about those who criticize President Trump for taking too long to share with the country the dire threats posed by the coronavirus. She began her answer this way: "What did he know, and when did he know it?" See Anna Palmer, Jake Sherman, Eli Okun, and Garrett Ross, "How to Think about Trump's Infrastructure Pitch," in *POLITICO Playbook PM*, posted March 31, 2020, https://www.politico.com/newsletters/playbook-pm/2020/03/31/how-to -think-about-trumps-infrastructure-pitch-4887622.

6. Goode, *The New Congress*, 51; Norman Ornstein et al., "Vital Statistics on Congress," Table 6-1 (Washington: Brookings, AEI, 2014), https://www.brookings .edu/wp-content/uploads/2016/06/Vital-Statistics-Chapter-6-Legislative -Productivity-in-Congress-and-Workload_UPDATE.pdf; and "Statistics and Historical Comparison: Bills by Final Status," GovTrack, https://www.govtrack.us /congress/bills/statistics.

7. James T. Currie, "The First Congressional Investigation: St. Clair's Military Disaster of 1791," *Parameters*, December 1990, 97, https://apps.dtic.mil/dtic/tr /fulltext/u2/a517709.pdf.

8. Currie, "The First Congressional Investigation," 100.

9. James Grant, *Mr. Speaker! The Life and Times of Thomas B. Reed, The Man Who Broke the Filibuster* (New York: Simon and Schuster, 2011), 71.

10. Neil MacNeil and Richard A. Baker, *The American Senate: An Insider's History* (New York: Oxford University Press, 2013), 240–41, 403n35.

11. Spenser S. Hue and Ann E. Marimow, "Former White House Counsel Don McGahn Does Not Have to Testify to House, Appeals Court Finds," *Washington Post*, February 28, 2020, https://www.washingtonpost.com/local/legal-issues/former -white-house-counsel-don-mcgahn-does-not-have-to-testify-to-house-appeals -court-finds/2020/02/28/eb846412-3c5a-11ea-baca-eb7ace0a3455_story.html.

12. For discussion of goal-oriented behavior of members of Congress and committee types, see Fenno, *Congressmen in Committees*; Deering and Smith, *Committees in Congress*. For a discussion on the importance of reelection as a goal and

the implications of that for the organization and workings of Congress, see David Mayhew, *Congress: The Electoral Connection*, 2nd ed. (New Haven, CT: Yale University Press, 2004).

13. Randall B. Ripley, *Power in the Senate* (New York: St. Martin's Press, 1969), 40–50.

14. The literature on the influence of committee chairs in this era is voluminous.

5

Congress and Political Parties

One of the challenges Congress faces is how to coordinate its members' activities. Like any other large organization, Congress needs to coordinate its members' activity in order to meet its responsibilities. Without having some way to organize its chambers and manage lawmakers' workloads, Congress would be hard pressed to write legislation, make decisions on the budget, and oversee the executive branch's implementation of the laws it enacts. It would also have a difficult time managing its relations with the president and the judiciary, with whom it shares power.

The Constitution says little about how all this is to be done. The framers, as noted in previous discussion, did establish presiding officers for each chamber. In the House of Representatives, it is the Speaker, who is selected by its members. In the Senate, the presiding officer is the vice president of the United States who, along with the president, is selected by the Electoral College. The Constitution, however, gives the Senate the authority to elect a president pro tempore (president for the time being) to serve in that role in the absence of the vice president. In addition, the framers included language in Article I of the Constitution that gives both chambers the authority to fill any other offices they might create. But apart from that, the framers said little about what any of these "other officers," or even their constitutionally designated presiding officers, would do in Congress.

This silence in the Constitution, coupled with each chamber's constitutional authority to determine "the Rules of its proceedings," left the first lawmakers free to make the decisions as to who would organize and guide their chambers' legislative business and how they would carry it out. The lawmakers responded to this challenge shortly after the first Congress convened. As they started to get the new government off the ground, creating executive branch departments and a federal court system as well as drafting a bill of rights, groups of lawmakers emerged to address the problem of managing Congress's work. These groups evolved and gradually crystallized into more stable coalitions or political parties. Once parties matured and gained acceptance as legitimate political structures, they became the primary vehicles through which Congress carried out its day-to-day work.

The term *congressional parties* in this context includes members of the House and Senate who belong to the same political party; so typically there are four congressional parties, two in each house of Congress. Today's congressional parties have created leadership structures and strategies to prioritize and conduct legislative activities, direct lawmakers, and coordinate relations with the executive branch. These parties help organize the institution and direct many of the lawmakers' behaviors. In today's more partisan Congress, parties have a decisive impact in shaping how individual members go about meeting their various congressional duties.

THE EMERGENCE OF CONGRESSIONAL PARTIES

Members of the founding generation of the United States had a deep distrust of political parties. They viewed them as factions or narrow sets of interests that, left unchecked, would upend their new republic. With that in mind, the Constitution's architects, as discussed in chapter 1, designed a system that would make it hard for majority factions to gain control of the national government and use it for narrow partisan ends. The framers raised concerns about the dangers factions or parties posed when they debated the merits of this new government in their ratifying conventions. The framers echoed those fears when they launched their new government. In his 1796 Farewell Address, President George Washington articulated those concerns as he counseled his fellow citizens to steer clear of the "spirit of party." Touching on themes that resonate in contemporary American life, he warned that this tendency to divide into parties "serves always to distract the public councils and enfeeble the public administration. It agitates the community with ill-founded jealousies and false alarms; kindles the animosity of one part against another; foments occasionally riot and insurrection. It opens the door to foreign influence and corruption, which finds a facilitated access to the government itself through the channels of party passion."[1]

Yet Washington was already too late when he raised his concerns about party divisions. By then, the partisan "spirit" he so deplored had already made its way into Congress and even his own administration. As discussed earlier, Washington's secretary of the treasury, Alexander Hamilton, worked with like-minded politicians, called the Federalists, to advance the administration's domestic policy initiatives within Congress. Many of those measures—including things like the national government's assumption of state debts, the creation of a national bank, and a sweeping economic program to promote the growth of the nation's manufacturing interests—promised to expand considerably the power of the central government. Washington's proposals, shaped to a large extent by Hamilton's analysis, alarmed many lawmakers, especially those who represented districts and states outside the more industrialized, northeastern part of the country. That group worried that Hamilton's proposals, if enacted, would transfer too much power away from the states. Led by James Madison, who worked closely with Washington's secretary of state, Thomas Jefferson, they responded by organizing congressional coalitions to block, derail, or slow down Hamilton's efforts. Thus, by the time Washington decided against standing for a third term as president, parties, in the form of loose alliances of members, had already emerged to provide some direction in how Congress carried out its work.[2]

Yet it would not be until the framers' generation passed from the political scene that parties routinely assumed responsibility for running Congress. By the 1830s, two parties emerged to dominate the nation's political landscape. They were the supporters of Andrew Jackson, better known as the Jacksonian Democrats, and his opponents, the Whigs. Each of these two parties, Democrats and Whigs, included politicians from all sections of the nation. Members within each party shared similar views on the role of the central government and policy. Democrats preferred more limited responsibilities for the national government while the Whigs endorsed a stronger central government that used its power to promote the development of the nation's infrastructure, including the building of roads, turnpikes, bridges, and canals. The two parties vigorously contested elections at all levels of government. By the time Jackson left the White House in 1836, the two parties were very much alive and well in Congress, and politicians had even come to accept them as necessary features of their republic.[3]

While the two-party system persisted, the parties that made it up changed considerably over the next half century. The Whigs could not survive internal divisions that erupted over the issue of slavery. The party broke into factions and was soon replaced by a new coalition of like-minded politicians, the Republican Party. After the Civil War and the era of Reconstruction, the parties gradually developed structures and offices to help them manage and run Congress. They did this as they adapted to changes in the political order brought about by industrialization, urbanization, and the settlement of the West. As a result, shortly after the turn of the twentieth century, the two major parties, Democrats and Republicans, had put in place outlines of the congressional party organization that we see today.

CONGRESSIONAL PARTY ORGANIZATIONS

Power in the congressional parties rests in the hands of both chambers' membership. In the House as well as the Senate, lawmakers exercise this power through party organizations known as caucuses or conferences. Democrats in both chambers use the term *caucus* while Republicans in both chambers use the term *conference*. It is in the House's and Senate's caucuses or conferences that congressional party members, shut away from the public and press, decide how they will organize, allocate authority among themselves, and plan how they will try to meet their partisan goals.

Shortly after the congressional elections, held in November every two years and before Congress opens in the first week of January, the two chambers' lawmakers gather separately in their caucuses and conferences to select their party leaders, consider changes to their own congressional party rules, and give final approval to the leadership's decisions on congressional committee assignments. Regular caucus and conference meetings during the year are held to make decisions on many of the procedures the parties will follow in carrying out their legislative business. At those sessions the parties debate, discuss, and make decisions about their policy agendas; collect and share information on their chambers' activities; and chart out their legislative and communications strategies.

Both chambers' parties select one of their members, generally a reliable supporter of the party, as chair of their caucus or conference. House and Senate Republicans and House Democrats single out one of their members specifically to do this job, while Senate Democrats assign the role to their floor leader. Conference and caucus chairs preside over party members' regular meetings, work with other members of their leadership teams to execute their party's decision, and facilitate communication between the leaders and the members. In recent years, chairs have also assumed greater responsibility for helping their members communicate to the public their party's message surrounding their legislative work.

Congressional parties have also established campaign committees to help them win elections. These organizations are the House's Democratic Congressional Campaign Committee and National Republican Congressional Campaign Committee and the Senate's Democratic Senatorial

Campaign Committee and the Republican Senate Campaign Committee. Campaign committees are chaired by a senior member of the party. Campaign committee chairs are charged with the responsibility of raising and distributing funds to help elect members of their party to Congress. They also work to recruit credible candidates to contest House and Senate seats in upcoming elections, and their offices provide strategic campaign support to candidates.

Both chambers' parties have committees that help them sort out their members' standing congressional committee assignments. These party committees, whose composition is determined by the party leadership, are known as steering committees for the House Republicans and House and Senate Democrats and committee on committees for the Senate Republicans. The two Senate parties also have separate policy committees, as do the House Republicans. House Democrats combine in one committee the work of a policy committee with that of its steering committee. Policy committees and the staff they employ provide party members research support and advice on selected policy issues. Frequently, they convene meetings where their party colleagues can learn about and discuss key issues emerging on the congressional agenda within their chambers.

ROLE OF CONGRESSIONAL LEADERSHIP

Selecting and allocating power to congressional party leaders are among the most important decisions conferences and caucuses make. Today's congressional party leaders are key players on the Hill. Their positions hold great power and prestige, and they serve the needs of the institution as well as those of their partisan colleagues.[4]

Leaders play an important role in making sure that 435 House members and 100 senators who represent a diverse array of districts and states across the country meet the constitutional responsibilities assigned to them collectively as the U.S. Congress. They are the ones who make the institution work. They are assisted by sizable staffs. Some staffers help them manage what happens inside their chambers, such as coordinating House activities, scheduling legislation, and getting out information to members and their staffs. Leaders also have aides who assist them with their work with other branches of government, their outreach to pressure groups, and their relations with the media.

Congressional leaders also serve institutional needs by controlling the flow of business on Capitol Hill. Those leaders set Congress's agenda, coordinate the work of its standing committees, and schedule legislation for floor debates and votes. They conduct negotiations and reach agreements between the two chambers on legislation and oversee executive branch activities, and they lead negotiations with members of the administration, including the president, to hammer out policy agreements between the executive and legislative branches of government.

In addition, congressional leaders help organize the Congress so that it can carry out its business. While both parties in the two chambers have steering committees or committees on committees to make decisions on assignments, leaders have a strong hand in determining who sits on what committees and who will lead each committee. Frequently, leaders use this as leverage to advance their party's interests. Members, after all, want seats on committees that will enable them to serve their constituents and get reelected. Some also want to be on committees where they can shape outcomes on policies that are of special interest to them. Some lawmakers even want slots on committees to gain greater prestige and clout on the Hill. Leaders can provide those, as they shape the composition of committees. In return, when leaders need a vote on an important piece of legislation in committees or on the floor, or support for a specific decision, they can usually rely on the member to deliver. Leaders also can take away an important committee assignment to punish members who either fail to provide sufficient support to the party on those issues that are especially important to it or flagrantly flout the party's prevailing expectations.

In addition to using their leverage to get members to support their parties' legislative goals, leaders also try to increase their parties' numbers on the Hill. Those in charge of the minority party, for instance, need to expand their membership to gain control of their legislative chambers so that they can advance their policy goals, while those in the majority want to keep and even expand their numbers. To obtain this electoral success, different members of the leadership teams often supplement their parties' campaign committees' work by lending a hand in fundraising activities. Frequently, they help candidates raise resources by attending their fundraisers, and they occasionally accompany candidates on the campaign trail to help them attract more attention and interest.

Finally, leaders play an important role in helping the congressional parties communicate their messages to the public. This role has taken on increased importance in roughly the last forty years. Before then, leaders concentrated their energies on what happened inside their chambers, bargaining with other members of Congress and the executive branch and manipulating rules and procedures to get things done. While those activities are still important parts of today's congressional leaders' job responsibilities, they must also be able to get their partisan messages out to the American people to build popular support for their efforts and improve their parties' standing with the public. Their goal is to shape the narrative in media outlets in ways that are favorable to their parties. This has taken on increased importance as presidents have devoted more time and resources to trying to build popular support for their policies by mounting more public appeals.[5]

As a result, congressional leaders frequently engage the media to defend their parties' legislative work and claim credit for their successes. Leaders also try to arrange public campaigns by rank-and-file members. To avoid sending the American people a muddled message, they try to make sure that their members strike the same chord in the same way and do so though the diverse array of media outlets that have appeared in recent years. Leaders accomplish this by providing members with themes or talking points they can use when they are interviewed by the media or having their staff supply members with material they can post on their digital platforms. As they have assumed the role of leading their parties' media messaging, these leaders frequently become targets of their partisan opponents. Speakers and Senate majority leaders in the era spanning the years 1930–1970, who wielded influence in quiet backroom negotiations with powerful committee chairmen, were often not widely known by many Americans. Since the 1990s, however, they have become the poster children of their partisan opponents' media campaigns and are regularly depicted as symbolic of what is supposedly wrong with their party's political agenda.

DIFFERENCES BETWEEN HOUSE AND SENATE LEADERSHIP

While House and Senate leaders perform many of the same duties, important differences set them apart. Senate leaders have less leverage over committee assignments, for instance. Because there are fewer of them, every senator usually sits on more than one major committee. While Senate leaders do have opportunities to weigh in on appointments and use those opportunities to reward or punish members of the party, their control is more limited than that of House leaders. It is also usually more difficult for Senate leaders to limit the impact of the chamber's minority party. The Senate's culture and rules allow individual senators greater freedom and influence. Because of its smaller size, history, and greater equality among its members, the Senate historically emphasizes deliberation over quick action and promotes decision-making by consensus. Its procedures give members great leeway to amend legislation and prolong debate on bills under consideration. Senate discussion and deliberation are so important that, under most conditions, stopping debate to bring legislation to the floor requires a supermajority of sixty votes. Those who lead the majority party in the Senate often find that they must make concessions both to members of their own party and members of the opposition to end debate and move things along. The flip side of this is that those who lead the minority party in the Senate have a greater ability to shape outcomes than do their counterparts in the House.

The House's structure and operations gives leaders of the majority party more leverage. Since it has so many members, it has over time adopted many rules and procedures that limit the behavior of individual members and give the Speaker considerable control over structuring how it goes about its day-to-day operation. This favors a cohesive majority party whose leaders can use these rules to limit minority party input and direct the behavior of their majority party colleagues.

HOUSE LEADERSHIP

Each House party's leadership team includes the chairs of the conference and caucus, congressional elections committees, and policy committees. In addition, there is an upper tier of leadership in both parties whose members manage, direct, and provide guidance and information to their rank-and-file partisan colleagues as they carry out their activities both inside and outside the chamber. Those members of the upper tier of leadership are the most influential and visible members of the two parties' leadership teams. For the majority party, these are the Speaker of the House, the majority leader, and the majority whip, and for the minority party, it is the minority leader and the minority whip.

Speaker of the House

The most important figure in the House of Representatives is the Speaker. While the entire House membership technically elects its Speaker before the start of each new Congress, the speakership is always filled, often on a strict party-line vote, by the majority party's candidate for the office.

As the House's only constitutional official, the Speaker's job extends beyond leading the majority party to include tending to the full chamber's needs. The Speaker oversees the House's administrative staff, presides over its proceedings, maintains decorum within the institution, performs certain ceremonial duties, and serves as the House's principal spokesperson.

Early Speakers generally refrained from playing an active political role. Even Henry Clay, who showed just how influential the office could become shortly after he gained the job in 1811, relied less on partisan tactics and more on his personality and skill to lead the House. The Speaker did not take on a more overtly partisan role until after the Civil War, when strong party organizations appeared on Capitol Hill.[6]

The powers and responsibilities of the Speaker have changed over time, often as a response to changes in party developments. As parties became stronger and more internally united in the post-Reconstruction era, they entrusted Speakers with more power. One of the first to benefit from this was Representative Thomas B. Reed of Maine. Backed by a unified House Republican majority party, he gained great leverage over the House during his tenure as Speaker in the 1890s. Reed skillfully used his influence over committee assignments and his control of procedures to shut down the opposition and successfully move his party's program through the House.

One of his Republican successors, Representative Joe Cannon of Illinois, followed Reed's example and used the office's powers aggressively to control House behavior. Yet as Cannon was exercising his power during the first decade of the twentieth century, changes were on the horizon. The election of several progressive, reform-minded Republican lawmakers from midwestern states created ideological divisions within his party. As noted in previous chapters, Cannon wielded power in a way that antagonized his party's reformers. This growing dissatisfaction set off a rebellion against his speakership. Progressive Republicans, who were miffed because the Speaker stifled their proposals, joined forces with House Democrats to strip away a lot of the Speaker's powers. By the time Cannon left office, the speakership was no longer the powerful office it had been before the revolt.

Speakers who followed Cannon still had considerable influence within the chamber, but they had to share power with committee chairs, who had gained increased leverage as the power of the Speaker declined. It was during this time that the committee chairs emerged as the pivotal figures on the Hill, the congressional "barons." In the House, the Speaker's ability to succeed depended on the ability to build support among the Speaker's ranks. Even Representative Sam Rayburn, a Democrat from Texas who held the office longer than any other person (serving seventeen years in the job on three different occasions from the end of the 1940s through the early 1960s) found that his success was, as one of his closest colleagues in the House put it, based "on personal influence rather than the structural power of the Speakership."[7]

Transformation in the parties in the 1980s had implications for the Speaker's role and powers. Changes in electoral voting patterns produced significant shifts in the composition of congressional parties. As many southern states started to replace conservative Democratic lawmakers with Republicans, the two parties became more unified internally and more ideologically opposed to one another. These changes prompted representatives and senators to grant more power to their leaders to accomplish the objectives that most of them shared.

The first clear signs that the environment on the Hill had shifted came in 1995. That was when Representative Newt Gingrich, a Republican from

Georgia, reclaimed the mantle of the speakership for his party after the Republicans gained control of the House for the first time in forty years. His party centralized power in the hands of the leadership—and particularly the Speaker—as a way of ensuring the House could deliver on the campaign promises Republicans had made during the 1994 midterm elections.

While the office of the Speaker has changed hands several times since then, both parties in the House now expect Speakers to use the office's formidable powers to advance their agenda when they are in control. Speakers who fail to meet these expectations run the risk of being toppled from office and replaced by other members of their party. For instance, House Republicans pressured several of the Speakers they put into office to step down because they had lost confidence in their leadership, including Gingrich (in 1998), Representative John Boehner of Ohio (2015), and Representative Paul Ryan of Wisconsin (2018), Even Representative Nancy Pelosi of California, who managed to reclaim the office of Speaker when her Democratic Party regained control of the House in 2018, had to work hard to quell dissent in the Democratic Caucus to stay on as Speaker. As part of her arrangement with her fellow Democrats, she agreed to step aside as Speaker in 2022, which in part is a sign of the power wielded by those members who are not entirely happy with her leadership.

In carrying out the role of leading the majority, the Speaker has many prerogatives that can be strategically used to support the party's agenda. The Speaker schedules the House's work and controls its proceedings. A Speaker has some leeway in determining what committee or committees will review proposed bills and can use that leverage to ensure that the proposals go to the committee or committees that are most likely to advance the party's objectives. The Speaker also appoints House members to conference committees to work out differences in legislation that has passed both chambers, and can use that power to influence outcomes. In addition, the Speaker also leads the House and controls its discussions in policy negotiations with the Senate as well as with members of the executive branch, including the president.

Within the party, the Speaker, in consultation with other members of the leadership team, shapes the party's standing-committee assignments and exercises great influence over the process of selecting committee chairs. By giving lawmakers coveted committee assignments that will enable them to realize their own political ambitions or goals, a Speaker can reward party members who support the majority on key floor votes. The Speaker also makes majority party appointments to the Rules Committee. The Speaker uses this power to ensure that the Rules Committee's decisions reflect the leadership's interest in controlling the conditions under which the full House takes up legislation. The Speaker works with other members of the leadership team to plan the party's policy agenda over the course of the legislative session and to develop and mount public relations strategies that enable the majority to communicate its message through the media in ways that help it advance initiatives inside the chamber and on the Hill. The Speaker also plays a major role in helping the congressional party raise money to support its candidates, and frequently heads out on the campaign trail to work on behalf of its candidates.

Majority Leader

The majority leader is arguably the House's second most influential member. Unlike the speakership, this position is not prescribed by the Constitution. It is instead a congressional party leadership position. The individual who holds this slot is chosen before the start of each Congress by the vote of the House majority party membership, not by the entire chamber, as is the case with the Speaker.

The majority leader position was not established until the late 1890s. Before then, different lawmakers within the party managed the majority's day-to-day floor activities. Frequently, the job fell to the chair of one of the key House money committees, either Appropriations or Ways and Means. In 1899, with the House controlled by the Republican Party, the Speaker formally named the chair of the Ways and Means Committee as the majority party's floor leader. When the Democrats gained control of the chamber twelve years later, in 1911, they opted to elect their floor leader, a practice that has been followed by both parties ever since.

Today, the party holding the House majority fills that slot with an established lawmaker who is well respected by most party members and who has demonstrated success in helping the party win elections and in communicating its message to the public. The majority leader is like a "field commander," who directly oversees the party's operations in the House.[8] The majority leader assists the Speaker in developing the majority party's agenda, shaping party members' committee assignments, and developing strategies to help the party attain its goals. The majority leader is especially involved in working with the chairs of committees, coordinating their work, guiding their activities, and working with the Speaker to schedule legislation they want to bring to the floor. The majority leader also provides party members with a broad overview of what is happening in Congress so that members stay informed about important legislative developments.

Minority Party Leader

The highest-ranking official in the minority party is the minority leader. This position was officially created at about the same time as that of the majority leader. The minority leader is elected by and heads the opposition in the House. Since a cohesive majority in the House of Representatives controls most of what happens in the chamber, the role of the minority leader is generally constrained unless the majority sees defections from its ranks. Because the majority party usually prevails in House decisions, the minority leader, at best, can only have a limited impact on what happens.

Still, the minority leader is entrusted with and exercises a great deal of clout within the party. The minority leader performs many important roles. These are primarily geared to keeping the party together in its opposition to the majority and carrying out efforts to reclaim control of the chamber. The minority party's leader will also work as a liaison to the executive branch when that party controls the presidency. The minority leader wields considerable power in parceling out committee assignments to its members. As is the case with the majority party leadership, the minority leader can build cohesion within the party by rewarding those members who support it with desired committee assignments. The minority leader also plays a key role in keeping members informed and in developing the minority party's policy alternatives to counter the majority's policy agenda. In addition, the minority leader assumes significant responsibility for mounting communications operations designed to get those policy positions across to the public. Like the majority, the minority needs to build public support for its positions and shape the news narrative in ways that work to its advantage. In fact, this public strategy is one of the few ways the minority party can have a significant impact, especially in the House, since the majority controls so many of that chamber's levers of power. Finally, the minority leader helps the party field and fund strong candidates so that it can win elections and gain back the majority, thus lending a hand to the party's congressional campaign committee.

Party Whips

Both parties established the position of party whip in 1897. The House Speaker at that time, Thomas Reed, needed help in gauging and rounding up support for legislation he wanted to bring to the floor for a vote, so he tapped someone in the party to assist him. Following Great Britain's House of Commons' parties' practice of enlisting party whips to keep their parties together on votes, the two parties gave this position that title. House Democrats, who were in the minority, followed suit and appointed a whip at the same time.

Today, both House parties' members elect their whips. In filling these slots, parties look to seasoned legislators who have an aptitude for figuring out where their own caucus and conference members stand on pending legislation and in keeping their party coalitions together. Since the majority party does not want to lose the vote on bills it brings to the House floor, the majority whip is expected to get a precise fix on how most of the party's regular members—often called the rank and file—intend to vote. The majority whip's job responsibilities also include being able to bargain with and convince wavering colleagues to support their party when they are needed to help pass important legislation. The minority whip works in concert with the minority leader to oppose the majority and keep the party together as it opposes the majority's initiatives. Both whips also help the leadership communicate with rank-and-file members about their strategies, both inside and outside the chamber. Both parties also enlist several members as part of a whip system to help the whips get information to the members and to round up votes on the floor when needed.

SENATE LEADERSHIP

The constitutionally designated presiding officer of the Senate is the vice president of the United States. In today's Congress, the vice president might help the administration by personally working to round up lawmakers' support for its programs and lobbying them on its behalf, but the vice president rarely presides over the Senate. Usually, the vice president only presides over the Senate if the chamber is evenly divided on a piece of legislation or on an executive or a judicial branch appointment, and the vice president is needed to break a tie by casting the deciding vote.

Most often, the vice president's role as presiding officer is filled by the president pro tempore of the Senate. The Senate's president pro tempore is elected by the membership. By tradition, the job goes to the majority party's most senior senator, with seniority measured by consecutive years of service in the Senate. Today, the office of president pro tempore is more symbolic than influential, though the occupant of the office is third in line in presidential succession, right behind the vice president and the Speaker of the House.

In practice, the chamber's most influential leadership figures are the congressional parties' two floor leaders and their whips, who in the Senate are commonly referred to as assistant party leaders. As is the case with party leaders in the House, assistant party leaders are all elected by their caucus and conference shortly after congressional elections, which are held every two years.

Like the House of Representatives, the Senate did not formalize party leadership positions until well after Reconstruction. As noted in chapter 2, for many years, small groups of highly respected senators who held key committee or party assignments controlled the chamber. Within this group, a senator frequently emerged to serve informally as the party's floor leader. That changed roughly a decade after the House established floor leaders and whips. While still in the minority, Senate Democrats created the position of whip in 1913 and elected their first leader in 1919. The Republicans soon followed suit. They created the whip position in 1915 and selected their first official floor leader in 1925.[9]

Today, the most powerful figure in the Senate is the majority leader. Selected by the party caucus or conference, majority leaders exercise influence over senators' committee assignments, including appointments to special committees. Majority leaders also help members gain access to resources needed to finance campaigns. They work with others in the conference or caucus to plan what will happen during the legislative session. They also shape chamber activities by determining the agenda, controlling the legislative schedule, and negotiating agreements with the minority to move legislation to the floor. The majority leader also plays a major role both in developing and communicating the party's message and in working with partisan colleagues to shape popular sentiment in ways that support the party's position. The majority leader also collaborates with the majority whip to keep the party together to move legislation to the floor and on to a successful vote. Finally, the majority leader plays an important role in negotiating legislation with House leaders and members of the executive branch, including the president.

Minority leaders head the opposition by working with others in their party to develop and present alternatives to the majority's agenda. The minority leader also uses influence over things like committee assignments and campaign resources and works with the minority whip to keep the party together in ways that enable it to counter or effectively reshape parts of the majority's legislative initiatives. The minority leader also works with the majority leader to reach agreements on moving legislation forward in the chamber. Because the Senate majority party frequently needs support from the minority to shut down debate and bring legislation to the floor, the minority leader can influence the process and even have some impact on the outcome. As one scholar noted, "Even when the majority is large, the Senate majority leader has no choice but to deal with the minority leader on a continuous basis."[10]

As with the House of Representatives, the fact that the contemporary Republican and Democratic Parties became more ideologically homogenous changed the set of expectations senators had for their chamber leaders. They wanted Senate leaders to play a more active role in shaping the Senate's work, and that is what those leaders did. Like their counterparts in the House, Senate leaders have responded to members' expectations by using the powers they have to advance their parties' legislative goals. Yet, given the institution's workings, structures, and procedures, Senate leaders frequently find themselves thwarted by what one former leader, Republican senator Howard Baker of Tennessee, described as the challenge of "trying to make ninety-nine independent souls act in concert under rules that encourage polite anarchy and embolden people who find majority rule a dubious proposition at best."[11]

PARTIES AND DECISIONS IN CONGRESS

While parties have, almost since the start of the American republic, played a major role in helping candidates get elected, organizing Congress, and guiding members' relations with other political actors, their imprint on policy outcomes has not been constant over time. The strong parties that emerged after the era of Reconstruction, for instance, resulted in significant policy differences between the parties. Those differences, combined with stronger leaders who aggressively pushed their policy agendas, brought about high levels of party-line voting in the two chambers—where a significant number of Democrats opposed a significant number of Republicans on many floor votes. The levels were considerably higher than they had been when the Whigs and Democrats did battle in Congress in the era before the Civil War. But that did not last long, for shortly after the turn of the twentieth century, things changed. The two parties became less cohesive and less polarized, while leaders lost a lot of their clout. While parties still played an important role on the Hill, they were no longer as sharply divided. House and Senate party-line voting on many policies declined as party chairs and other influential members worked inside the party and across the aisle to craft policy outcomes that would pass both chambers with bipartisan majorities.

Yet that cooperation across party lines also proved to be short lived. Changes in the electorate over the course of the twentieth century, especially in southern states, resulted in a sorting out of the parties. As they became more internally united and polarized, the parties entrusted their leaders with more power and expected them to use that power aggressively to advance their partisan agendas. More cohesive and polarized parties, combined with stronger and more assertive ideological leaders, have dramatically increased recent party-line voting, reaching levels that have rarely been seen in roughly three-quarters of a century.[12] The institutionalization of such bitter partisan opposition can complicate the work that Congress needs to do as it legislates and interacts with the other branches of government.

CONCLUSION

Political parties play an important role in helping Congress meet its constitutional responsibilities. Though initially a source of concern to the framers' generation, political parties have become important vehicles though which Congress carries out its work. They make it possible for individual members of the House and the Senate, who reflect the interests of a diverse range of districts and states across the nation, to come together to write legislation and manage the institution's relations with the other branches of government. Though not mentioned in the Constitution, parties enable Congress to manage its legislative work and carry out its oversight responsibilities. It is through them that Congress responds to the demands of the American people, represents their interests, makes policy decisions, and oversees the work of the executive branch. And it is through them that Congress is held accountable for its work. In doing all of this, congressional parties, much like other parts of the institution, have proven to be dynamic. They have adapted to changes on the larger political landscape and have adjusted their organizational structures and strategies to meet the changing needs of members over time.

NOTES

1. George Washington, "Farewell Address," in *American Political Thought*, eds. Isaac Kramnick and Theodore Lowi (New York: W. W. Norton, 2019), 279.

2. See Joanne Barrie Freeman, "Opening Congress," in *The American Congress: The Building of Democracy*, ed. Julian E. Zelizer (New York: Houghton Mifflin, 2004), 25–37.

3. Joel H. Silbey, "Congress in a Partisan Era," in *The American Congress: The Building of Democracy*, ed. Julian E. Zelizer (New York: Houghton Mifflin, 2004), 142.

4. The discussion of the role of party leaders relies on Roger H. Davidson, Walter J. Oleszek, Frances E. Lee, and Eric Schickler, *Congress and Its Members*, 16th ed. (Thousand Oaks, CA: CQ Press, 2018), chap. 6. For a historical overview of leaders in the Senate, see Randall B. Ripley, *Power in the Senate* (New York: St. Martin's Press, 1969).

5. Samuel Kernell, *Going Public: New Strategies of Presidential Leadership* (Washington, DC: CQ Press, 1997); and Gary Lee Malecha and Daniel J. Reagan, *The Public Congress: Congressional Deliberation in a New Media Age* (London: Routledge Press, 2012).

6. Ronald M. Peters Jr., *The American Speakership: The Office in Historical Perspective*, 2nd ed. (Baltimore, MD: Johns Hopkins University Press, 1997), 35–40; see also chapter 2 for a discussion of the rise of a "partisan speakership."

7. Richard Bolling, *Power in the House: A History of the House of Representatives* (New York: Capricorn Books, 1974), 190. See also Peters, *The American Speakership*, chaps. 1, 2, and 3.

8. Walter J. Oleszek, "The Role of the House Majority Leader: An Overview," *CRS Report for Congress*, April 4. 2006, http://www.congressionalresearch.com /RL30665/document.php.

9. Neil MacNeil and Richard A. Baker, *The American Senate: An Insider's History* (New York: Oxford University Press, 2013), chap. 7; and Ripley, *Power in the Senate*.

10. Barbara Sinclair, "Senate Parties and Party Leadership, 1960–2010," in *The U.S. Senate: From Deliberation to Dysfunction*, ed. Burdette A. Loomis (Washington, DC: CQ Press, 2012), 106.

11. MacNeil and Baker, *American Senate*, 229.

12. Bryan W. Marshall and Bruce C. Wolpe, *The Committee: A Study of Policy, Power, Politics and Obama's Historic Legislative Agenda on Capitol Hill* (Ann Arbor: University of Michigan Press, 2018), 205.

6

The Legislative Process

To become a law, a bill must be passed in the same form by the House and the Senate and then signed by the president. Moreover, the bill must be approved by all three during the same Congress in which it is introduced. Each Congress meets for two yearlong sessions and is numbered in the order in which it was convened, starting with the First Congress (1789–1791). Each new Congress begins its first session at noon on January 3 of each odd-numbered year after a general national election, unless the previous Congress specifies a different starting date.

Members of Congress introduce a combined total of about ten thousand bills every year, yet usually only about 3–4 percent of them will survive to become law during a single Congress. Of those, a few are laws that must be passed every year. These include bills that do things such as fund governmental activities or raise the ceiling on the national debt. Meanwhile, many of the others that do succeed involve primarily ceremonial, noncontroversial actions that are usually approved by Congress with little opposition. Such measures, which in recent years have accounted for nearly a third of all public bills passed by Congress, include things such as naming a federal courthouse after someone or approving a special postage stamp or coin to honor a person or to commemorate a significant historical event. What all this means is that many significant legislative proposals die some place on Capitol Hill.[1]

One reason so many bills fail to become law is because the legislative process is so complicated. As this chapter shows, even under the best of conditions, the course that a bill must run from its introduction to getting signed by the president faces many hurdles that can either slow it down or trip it up entirely. Absent a crisis demanding an immediate congressional response, the process creates delays, frustrates lawmakers, and yields results that satisfy few.

To a certain extent, slow and deliberate governmental action is what the framers had in mind when they drafted the Constitution. Sensitive to the dangers posed by strong, centralized governmental power, they did not want to establish a legislative branch that was too energetic or moved too swiftly. They instead preferred an institution that would represent different perspectives and sentiments and encourage the exchange of ideas and negotiation and compromise in responding to the nation's problems and advancing its interests. They recognized that differences within the chambers, as well as those between them, would make agreement difficult, and that aspect, they believed, was not such a bad thing. As Alexander Hamilton observed in *Federalist 70*, "In the legislature, promptitude of decisions is oftener an evil than a benefit. The differences of opinion, and the jarrings of parties in that department of the government, though they may sometimes obstruct salutary plans, yet often promote deliberation and circumspection, and serve to check excesses in the majority."[2]

As the House and Senate evolved, they developed different rules and procedures to govern their work. Because it had far more members, the House of Representatives established more rules and formal procedures than the Senate did, and it gradually added to those over time. These regulations guide and direct how individual representatives behave as the House conducts its business, and they allow that chamber to more effectively manage its workload. The Senate, because it was a smaller body, did not need so many constraints on its individual members to get its collective work done. Thus it allowed them more leeway as they conducted their legislative business, and that pattern has continued to evolve.

All of this has important implications for today's Congress. The House provides its members with less freedom and flexibility, and when it is controlled by a cohesive majority, the chamber's extensive rules allow it to direct the flow of business within the chamber. This gives majority party leaders like the Speaker of the House of Representatives opportunities to intervene in the legislative process to shape what happens within the chamber. In contrast, the Senate is an institution in which individual members can play a greater role and have more impact, even if members of the majority party stick together. It is an institution that generally allows greater flexibility and requires more accommodation and agreement from its members to reach a decision that a majority is willing to support. Yet the increased partisanship in the contemporary Senate allows its leaders to play a more active role in shaping legislative outcomes than was the case in the middle decades of the last century.[3]

INTRODUCTION OF BILLS

Ideas for bills come from many different sources. Sometimes constituents suggest to a senator or representative an idea for new legislation to address a problem they have experienced or encountered that requires governmental action. Interest groups are another source of legislative ideas for lawmakers. Some of them even go so far as to write the language to be included in a proposed bill that will directly affect them. Ideas for bills also come from staff members who work for lawmakers or congressional committees. Members of the executive branch, such as a cabinet officer or the head of an administrative agency or bureau, also bring to the attention of Congress issues that need to be addressed or proposals that they favor and want to see enacted into law. This includes the president, who is given the constitutional authority to "recommend" to Congress "such measures as he shall judge necessary and expedient." Starting with President Woodrow Wilson, it has become common for Speakers to invite presidents to deliver their State of the Union address in the House chamber in front of all senators and representatives, and presidents frequently highlight their legislative proposals in those talks. Finally, lawmakers themselves also come up with policies that they would like to see Congress adopt. These may come out of work that they are doing on a committee, or they may emerge because of problems that directly affect their states or districts. Some members of Congress also have special expertise or an abiding interest in a policy that they would like to advance in legislation during their time on the Hill.

Regardless as to where the idea for a legislative proposal comes from, all bills, including those that originate directly from the White House, must be introduced by a member of Congress. The senator or representative who introduces a bill is referred to as its sponsor. Frequently, the bill's sponsor will try to get other lawmakers in the sponsor's chamber to sign on as cosponsors. A bill that has many cosponsors signals to other colleagues that it has broad support, thus increasing its chances in the chamber in which it is introduced. Lawmakers who agree to be a bill's cosponsor gain something as well. They can use their cosponsorship of legislation to beef up their record, gain media attention, attract interest-group support, and provide voters back home with evidence that they are engaged in their legislative work. That can come in handy when they seek reelection or pursue another elective office in the future.

Members in today's Congress often try to increase a bill's chance of success by giving it a snappy title or acronym to attract the public's interest and shape popular sentiment on the legislation. One classic case here is a law passed shortly after the September 11, 2001, terrorist attacks that gave the federal government an array of sweeping powers to investigate and deter terrorist activity. Officially called the Uniting and Strengthening America by Providing Appropriate Tools Required to Intercept and Obstruct Terrorism Act, it is often referred to as the USA PATRIOT Act. Such an acronym captures the media's interest, links the bill to something that is symbolically attractive, and is easy for most people to remember. It also frames legislation in a way that makes it difficult to table or oppose, since most members of Congress would find themselves hard pressed to oppose legislation that is supportive of patriotism. Other examples of recent bills and their creative acronyms include the Brewers Excise and Economic Relief Act, or the BEER Act; the Jumpstarting Our Business Sector Act, or the JOBS Act; and the Robo Call Off Phones Act, or the Robo COP Act.[4]

In the House of Representatives, the sponsor formally introduces a bill by putting a physical copy of it into the legislative hopper, a wooden box attached to the House clerk's desk. Bills are introduced in the Senate by presenting them to one of the chamber's legislative clerks or by introducing them directly from the chamber floor. The same legislative proposal can be introduced simultaneously in both chambers, though each one must consider it separately. The only exception involves bills that raise or spend money. The Constitution requires that all bills raising revenue—that is, tax legislation—start in the House; and by practice, all bills spending money usually start there as well.

Once a bill has been introduced, it is given a number. Bills are numbered in the order in which they come in, though the party that controls the chamber occasionally reserves certain numbers for bills. It may, for example, use lower numbers for bills that are especially important to it and its supporters. Bills are labeled according to the chamber in which they start, the House of Representatives (H. R.) or Senate (S.), followed by the number assigned to them. Examples would be H. R. 1 and S. 1. The two chambers may also take up what are known as joint resolutions. These are labeled with the prefixes H. J. Res. or S. J. Res. depending on where they start. Joint resolutions are like bills, though they may be narrower in scope as to what they do. Joint resolutions are used, for example, to provide emergency funding in the wake of national disasters, such as hurricanes or earthquakes or pandemics, such as the spread of the coronavirus (COVID-19).

Congress will occasionally pass two other types of resolutions, neither of which requires the president's signature or becomes law if passed. The first one is a concurrent resolution: H. Con. Res. or S. Con. Res. Concurrent resolutions are used to address procedures of both houses. Congress, for example, uses concurrent resolutions on the budget to guide its committees' annual decisions on spending and raising revenue. Concurrent resolutions are also used to express the institution's views on an issue or to commemorate an important historical event. In 2019, Congress passed a concurrent resolution that recognized the Armenian Genocide by the Ottoman Empire that took place between 1915 and 1923. The other type of resolution, the H. Res. or S. Res., is one passed by a single chamber. These simple resolutions are often used to address the procedures or rules of the legislative body that passes them. Like concurrent resolutions, they can also be employed by either the House or the Senate to indicate its members' views or sentiments on a specific item, action, event, or person. They have, for instance, been used by a chamber to reprimand one of its members for ethics violations or other misdeeds.

After a bill is assigned a number, it is referred to one or more committees in the chamber in which it was introduced. The authority to make this decision rests with the chamber's presiding officer, though in practice it is the parliamentarian of each body who, based on the bill's title and subject matter, determines what committee will take it up. Sometime a bill's subject matter is too broad to fit within a single committee's domain. In those instances when a bill's subject matter cuts across the jurisdiction of many different committees, it may be referred to more than one committee, a process known as multiple referral. Multiple referral is more common in the House than in the Senate. When multiple referral is used, one committee is designated as having primary responsibility for the bill, though in today's more partisan Congress, leaders of the majority party will exercise great control in coordinating and even directing the work of the different committees involved. Sometimes they even get directly involved in writing the bill themselves and making many of the important decisions that would have been otherwise left to committees. This happens on legislation they identify as a high priority for the party, and it has become more common in the last twenty-five years, as leaders have increased their leverage on the Hill.

THE DECISION TO TAKE UP THE BILL

One of the first obstacles that can slow down or derail a bill is getting the assigned committee to act on it. Most bills that arrive in committees are never taken up but are instead left to die. There are many reasons why this happens. Sometimes there are other bills that are more pressing and need to be finished before Congress ends its work or adjourns. In other cases, there may not be adequate interest or support in the committee to take up the bill. The chair of the committee may not consider it to be a priority item or believe that it is not the right time to move the legislation through the committee. Majority chamber leaders can also intervene to kill the bill. They may conclude that there is not enough support for it within the party or that moving it forward would create serious divisions within the party. Interest groups opposed to the legislation may also step up their campaigns to pressure committee members to table a bill. It is also possible that the sponsor of the legislation has only introduced the bill to keep a constituent or interest group happy and does not really want to spend the political capital necessary to move the bill forward.

Both chambers have ways to pry bills out of committees that fail to act on a legislative proposal. In the House of Representatives, the most significant procedural mechanism for doing this is to file a discharge petition. A discharge petition requires the signature of 218 members—a majority—to get a bill out of committee and bring it to the floor for a vote. Yet getting a majority to support a discharge petition is not an easy task. Lawmakers are not inclined to challenge colleagues on other committees. Some fear that if they use a discharge petition to upend the decision of another committee, they may face a similar challenge in their own committees. Leaders of the majority party also put a lot of pressure on members not to oppose decisions made by the committees, which are effectively under their control. While some representatives occasionally threaten to file a discharge petition to force a committee to report a bill to the floor for a vote, most of these efforts fail to get the required number of signatures.

The Senate also has a discharge process. But its rules provide members with other, easier ways to advance legislation that is held up in committee. For instance, a senator can take a proposal that is ignored in one committee and offer it as an amendment to a different bill that is being considered on the floor. Unlike House members, a senator can introduce amendments that are not related to or germane to the content of the legislation that is under consideration. A senator, for example, can take education legislation that is tied up in one committee and offer it as an amendment to a bill on agriculture that the chamber is debating. There are a couple of exceptions to this. Nongermane amendments cannot be made to some types of legislation, such as budget reconciliation bills. The Senate, as will be discussed later, can also reach unanimous consent agreements that restrict amendments. These are crafted and agreed to before they begin debating a bill.

Senate rules also make it possible for members to use special procedures to bypass committees entirely. Under certain conditions, they can put a bill directly on the chamber's calendar for debate and a vote. Senators can employ this strategy if they fear that a bill will be sent to a committee that will bottle it up or not move fast enough on it.

HEARINGS ON LEGISLATION

After receiving and reviewing a bill, if a committee wants to move it forward the committee chair will usually schedule a round of hearings. Today, most committee hearings are open to the public, and Congress keeps a record of what happens at them. Transcripts of these sessions are published by the government and are made available online. Hearings may be conducted by the entire committee itself or by one or more of its more specialized subcommittees, which will focus on specific topics in the legislation over which they have jurisdiction. Depending on the committee, the scope of the legislation, and the preferences of the committee chair and the party leaders, hearings may be held by both the subcommittees and the full committee.

In convening hearings, committees and subcommittees invite people to testify on the bill. They do this so that they can amass information to make an informed decision on the merits of the proposed legislation and how it might be improved. Committee members and party leaders also use hearings to gauge the level of political support for, or opposition to, the proposed legislation. Frequently the people called to testify at these sessions include leaders of interest groups, academics, members from think tanks or research organizations, and other expert witnesses, as well as officials from other levels of government and the executive branch and congressional staff. Witnesses might even include some constituents who have a stake in the proposed legislation. Some members of Congress with expertise in subject matter covered by the bill might be called to share their views on the legislation as well. Occasionally, subcommittees and committees even bring celebrities who have a special interest in a topic to Capitol Hill to testify at their hearings. They sometimes do this to attract media attention to the issue so that they can build public support that will help them move the bill forward. Rock stars, movie actors, professional athletes, and comedians have testified at hearings to discuss issues and legislation important to them; they include U2's Bono, Seth Rogen, Jon Stewart, Ben Affleck, Julia Roberts, Michael J. Fox, Muhammad Ali, Oprah Winfrey, and even Sesame Street's Elmo.

Once they finish their hearings, subcommittees and committees take up the work of revising the bill. This stage of the legislative process is known as markup. Committee members revise, or "mark up," the bill's provisions after considering information gathered through hearings and consultations with staff. Members of the committee staff who have substantial expertise in the policy area that the committee covers provide important guidance and technical advice and help resolve problems that emerge during the committee's deliberations. Lawmakers negotiate and vote on changes they want to make, and they work with committee staff and even members of the administration and lobbyists to finalize the bill's legislative language. This is followed by considerable discussion and debate between members. If hearings are held at the subcommittee level, its members will vote on forwarding their work to the full committee. The full committee then has the option of either holding additional hearings on the bill and marking it up and then voting on it or simply agreeing to accept the subcommittees' decisions. Either way, unless the committee decides to postpone taking any action, it will vote on moving the bill out of committee.

The increased partisanship and polarization of today's Congress sometimes complicate committee actions and undermine its deliberative process, especially in the House of Representatives, where the majority party has greater leverage and uses it to its advantage. As parties have become more cohesive and opposed to one another in recent years, the minority party frequently finds it has a hard time influencing what a committee does. Occasionally, a minority party might even opt to steer clear of committee deliberations and the process of marking up legislation. For example, when Democrats considered the Affordable Care Act—also known as Obamacare—in 2010, many House Republicans, with the blessing of their party leaders, refused to participate in committee discussions and markup sessions.

When the committee votes out a bill, it files an accompanying report that is prepared by committee staff members. This report usually includes the committee's recommendations, a summary of the legislation, a record of the decisions it made, and the reasons why it decided the way that it did. Those who oppose the legislation can have staff members include their objections to the bill as well. Reports provide important information to other lawmakers in the chamber as well as individual constituents, lobbyists, pressure groups, and other governmental officials who have a special interest in the legislation. Committee reports also become part of the bill's legislative history that can be used to guide others—administrators and the courts—in interpreting the legislation if it is signed into law.

Even after the legislation has been voted out of committee, leaders of the majority party frequently intervene to make additional adjustments to the bill. After the committee finishes its work, they gauge support for the legislation in their caucus or conference. They want to make sure they have enough backing from rank-and-file members for it to pass. If they discover that they are falling short of the threshold required, they will negotiate with members and revise provisions of the legislation until they win their support. These changes, known as postcommittee adjustments, are now more common on major pieces of legislation in both chambers.[5]

SCHEDULING LEGISLATION

Once they believe they have enough support to move the legislation to the floor, leaders in the majority party begin working out arrangements to debate and vote on the legislation. In the House of Representatives, the Speaker plays a major role in scheduling when legislation will come up for consideration.

The House has several procedures for acting on minor and ceremonial bills. Such legislation is usually noncontroversial and is easily dispensed with by the House either through a "suspension of the rules" or through unanimous consent, both of which generally require some support from the minority party. Debate is restricted to forty minutes, and no amendments are allowed under suspension of the rules; in addition, a two-thirds majority is needed to pass legislation treated in this fashion. Bringing legislation up under unanimous consent requires the approval of leadership in both parties as well as the chairs and ranking minority members of the committee or committees that considered the legislation.

Most major pieces of legislation in the House follow a different route. They are sent to the Rules Committee before being scheduled for debate and a floor vote. The Rules Committee is one of the most important standing committees in the House of Representatives, and it serves the interests of the majority party. The Speaker selects the members of the majority party who will sit on the committee and uses that prerogative to shape the composition of the committee and exercise control over it. By controlling appointments and through frequent consultations with the committee's chair, the Speaker can influence the committee's decisions in ways that advance the majority party's political and policy goals.

The Rules Committee has the power to decide the rules of debate that will be followed when legislation is taken up by the whole chamber. After holding a round of hearings on the legislation, the committee, depending on the Speaker's instructions, will vote to give the bill an open or a closed rule. An open rule can take different forms, but it generally allows for more discussion and amendments on a bill as it is considered by the House. Such a rule makes it possible for the minority party to play a role in debating and amending a bill and shaping its outcome.

Closed rules, in contrast, impose many more restrictions on what the minority party can do to a bill. While closed rules can take on a variety of forms, they generally do three things: they limit legislative debate, restrict the types of amendments that can be offered to a bill, and determine how those amendments will be voted on by the House. Some versions of closed rules even forbid amendments. Closed rules can be used to speed things up, limit deliberation, and determine outcomes. In recent years, as the Congress has become more partisan and polarized, Speakers have increasingly used the Rules Committee to restrict input from the minority, to ensure that the majority party gets what it wants and does not have to cast votes on amendments that might be politically difficult for its members.

Given the Senate's rules and the greater leeway granted to its members, the majority party has less control over scheduling legislation for debate and a vote. House rules enable a cohesive majority to exercise significant control over its work to a degree that Senate rules do not provide. But individual senators have many chances to slow down or even kill legislative proposals. This is because the Senate allows unlimited debate on all but a few types of legislation such as budgetary reconciliation bills. This delaying tactic of what in the past was referred to as "talking a bill to death" is known as a filibuster.

THE FILIBUSTER

The possibility of a filibuster also permits a senator to place a hold on a legislative proposal. A hold takes place when a senator informs the leadership that the senator may filibuster the legislation or object to its going forward. That can also slow things down or bring them to a halt. Leaders can refuse to honor a senator's request for a hold, but there are some costs associated with denying such requests. Denials can lead to long delays as members work out agreements on how exactly to bring a bill to the floor, and even then, they may face a filibuster.

The only way to end a filibuster on legislative debates is through a vote of cloture. The Senate first introduced a cloture rule in 1917. It did that after President Woodrow Wilson publicly upbraided senators—"a little group of willful men, representing no opinion but their own"—for filibustering a bill he wanted Congress to put on his desk for him to sign. An overwhelming number of senators agreed with Wilson's view, and they responded by adopting a cloture provision that made it possible for a supermajority of two-thirds of senators present to cut off debate.[6] In 1975, the Senate modified the rule and reduced to sixty the number of votes required to end debate.

In 2013, the Republican-controlled Senate eliminated the use of filibusters for confirming nominees to the courts and the executive branch. But it is a tool that can be used by senators under most circumstances when that chamber considers legislation, and it is still very difficult to end debate by invoking closure. Even with the lower threshold of sixty votes, the majority party almost always come up short. From 1976 to 2020, there have only been four years when the Senate majority party held a filibuster-proof majority of sixty senators. Because the majority party by itself rarely has enough votes to prevail on a cloture vote, it must round up some support from the opposition, something that is not easy to do in today's more partisan environment.

The Senate's filibuster has a long and fabled history. For many years, a senator or group of senators mounted a filibuster by going to the floor and speaking for hours on end. This frequently brought the entire institution to a halt, because Senate rules kept them from taking up anything else. When he was in the Senate, Huey Long, a Democrat from Louisiana, once held up the Senate's work by staging a more than fifteen-hour-long filibuster against a provision in one of President Franklin Delano Roosevelt's New Deal bills. As part of his marathon address, he read and analyzed the U.S. Constitution and recited recipes for fried oysters and "potlikker," the juice left behind after boiling mustard or turnip greens and a pound of "side meat" in water. The longest filibuster on record was the one mounted by then Democratic senator Strom Thurmond, from South Carolina. Thurmond deployed the tactic to try to kill a civil rights bill in 1957. He held the floor for more than twenty-four hours. Though frequently portrayed by its supporters as a procedure to protect the interests of the minority and to foster deliberation, filibusters in the mid-twentieth century were most often deployed by southern Democratic senators like Thurmond to delay or kill civil rights bills. Yet apart from those efforts aimed to undermine civil right bills, Senate filibusters were not common events in the mid-twentieth century, and prevailing norms discouraged their use.

Today, filibusters and cloture votes are common in the Senate. But they no longer grind the whole institution to a halt, and senators rarely take to the floor to talk. In the mid-1970s, the Senate instituted procedural reforms that made it possible to consider other legislation while a bill was being filibustered. This "two-track system" keeps the Senate up and running even during a filibuster, since it can continue its work on other matters. This change thus narrows a filibuster's impact. But since senators do not have to actually spend their time talking on the floor, it also encourages members to use it more often. Today, simply the threat of mounting a filibuster makes it hard for the Senate to complete work on the targeted bill. This gives the minority some leverage. It also lets individual senators from either party extract concessions on bills. As the number of filibusters has increased in recent years, so has the number of motions to invoke cloture. Today in the Senate, the "default assumption" is that legislative proposals "can only pass if supporters can muster sixty votes to invoke cloture on them."[7] Because this supermajority is hard to reach, the Senate fails to pass a lot of legislation approved by the House. And when it does act, it usually does so with input provided by the minority party, something that is frequently absent in today's House.

The most common way to avoid a filibuster and advance legislation to the Senate floor is through a unanimous consent agreement. A unanimous consent agreement is hammered out between the Senate's majority and minority leaders as well as other interested members. The agreement may also include input from the chair and ranking minority member of the committee that considered the legislation as well as from other committee members who have a special interest in the bill. Unanimous consent agreements require a broad consensus from senators of the two political parties, since they must be approved by the Senate without objection. Unanimous consent agreements will specify conditions as to how the legislation will be debated and amended. They will often specify what amendments will be offered and when they will be debated and voted on, and they will usually include time limits on getting these things done. On major pieces of legislation, a unanimous consent agreement, which is binding on all members, is like a rule granted by the House Rules Committee.[8]

DEBATE AND VOTE

House majority leaders, particularly the Speaker, determine when legislation will be brought up for a vote. Each party selects a representative to manage the bill when it comes up for discussion. Usually, these floor managers are the chair of the committee reporting the bill and the ranking minority member on that committee. They lead their party's debate. They also allot speaking time on it to members of their parties.

The first order of business for a more complicated, major piece of legislation that is brought to the floor is the adoption of the rule given to it by the Rules Committee. As noted earlier, this rule sets down conditions for debating and amending the bill. After debate, the House votes on the rule and almost always accepts it on a strict party-line vote. Though it sometimes happens, losing a vote on the rule is rare. The expectation is that even those in the majority who do not intend to vote for the legislation will support the party in a vote on the rule. This expectation reflects the fact that leaders can mount considerable pressure on their partisan colleagues to make sure that they back their party.

After adopting the rule, the House resolves itself into the Committee of the Whole to debate and amend the bill. The Committee of the Whole includes all House members, but it only requires one hundred representatives to make up a quorum. A member of the majority party other than the Speaker presides over its proceedings, which are carried out according to "rules that are designed to speed up floor action and facilitate debate."[9] Voice votes are allowed in the Committee of the Whole, though electronically recorded votes are required if twenty-five members request them.

During floor debate, representatives who speak on the bill stride up to one of the two lecterns in the well of the House chamber. There they deliver their brief remarks, with Democrats speaking from the lectern on the left and Republicans speaking from the one on the right. Representatives often use speaking time allotted to them by the floor managers to frame how the legislation will be interpreted by the media and the general public. They do that by repeating specific themes or talking points about the legislation provided to them in advance by their party leaders. Once they finish their remarks, House members debate and vote on amendments, provided such changes are allowed under the adopted rule. As noted earlier, the majority party leaves little to chance during this phase by considering most major pieces of legislation under closed rules that impose strict limits on amendments.

The House dissolves the Committee of the Whole after it has finished discussing and amending the bill, and the Speaker returns to the rostrum to preside over the full House, which requires 218 members for a quorum, for the last votes. House rules give the minority party an opportunity to introduce a motion to send the bill back to committee. This motion to recommit the legislation, which would effectively kill it, is usually defeated by the majority party. The minority's motion to recommit is then followed by a final vote, with House members recording their votes electronically during the voting period, which must last for at least fifteen minutes. Occasionally when things look close, party leaders keep applying pressure all the way through to the end to make sure that they keep as many of their rank-and-file members in line as possible.

Senate debate and amendments are usually governed by the provisions of unanimous consent agreements worked out and adopted by the parties. These must be agreed to by all senators. They are also binding on all of them. Without a unanimous consent agreement, the chamber's rules allow virtually any amendment to be offered, including those that are not germane to the legislation, and they allow for unrestricted debate that can only be shut down through a successful cloture vote.

After the Senate accepts the provisions of the unanimous consent agreement, the bill is scheduled for debate and amendments. While unanimous consent agreements establish conditions for the consideration of the legislation in the Senate, debates and votes on amendments in that chamber are still a bit more freewheeling and open than they are in the House. During the debate and amendment stage, the legislation is managed by each party's floor managers, usually the chair and ranking minority member of the primary committee that filed a report on the legislation. After debate and votes on amendments, the clerk calls the roll, and senators announce their final vote on the bill.

CONFERENCE AND FINAL VOTE

The two chambers rarely pass a bill in the same form. The Constitution requires, however, that a bill cannot be sent to the president for signature into law if there are any differences between the version passed by the House and the version passed by the Senate. The chambers must therefore find a way of resolving the differences between the two versions. In the past, Congress routinely did this by sending the bill to a conference committee. A conference committee includes members from both chambers. The conferees are usually from the committees that initially reported the legislation and they are selected by congressional leaders to represent their parties, though sometimes the leaders themselves get directly involved. In today's more partisan environment, the Speaker and the majority leader of the Senate might even shut out minority members from the conference's deliberations.

Conferees from each chamber meet to address the differences between the two bills. Normally, they receive instructions on negotiations from the chamber they represent, and congressional rules do place some limits on the types of changes they can make. They cannot, for instance, add anything that was not included in either of the versions of the legislation, nor can they eliminate provisions or items that both chambers included in their separate bills. In their negotiations, the conferees are mindful of what the two chambers will support when asked to approve their committee's final product. What they agree to is known as a conference report, and to become law it must be voted on and adopted by both houses.

Another, increasingly more prevalent, way of working out the differences between the chambers on a bill is through a "ping-ponging" process. Legislative ping-ponging involves sending the bill back and forth between the House and Senate. The two chambers, guided by majority party leaders, keep amending the bill and sending it back and forth to one another until they finally reach an accord. When one party controls both chambers, ping-ponging gives leaders of the majority greater leverage in shaping the final product to be sent to the president.[10]

In casting their vote to pass the legislation, members of Congress keep in mind a wide range of different factors. These include how the legislation will affect their constituencies as well as concerned interests that may be important to them. They do not want to offend those folks who elect them and who provide them with campaign funding and assistance when they seek reelection. Members on both sides and in both chambers are also attentive to the demands of their party. In today's Congress, as parties have become more cohesive and polarized, most members are likely to share common ideological bonds and policy preferences. As a result, party-line voting has climbed to very high levels in recent years.[11]

SENDING BILLS TO THE PRESIDENT

Once the two chambers have reached an agreement on all the provisions of a bill, the legislation is formally printed and signed by the two chambers' presiding officers. The bill is now considered enrolled, and it is sent or "presented" to the president. This is the final hurdle that a bill must surmount to become law. According to Article I, Section 7, Clause 2, of the Constitution, the president can sign the bill and it becomes law. The Constitution guarantees presidents ten days (excluding Sundays) to consider such bills, and if after that time the president takes no action, the bill automatically becomes law. If Congress adjourns before the ten days are up, the president can sign the bill or can take no action and kill the bill, which is known as a pocket veto.

The president can also reject the proposed legislation by vetoing it. The Constitution states that if the president vetoes the bill, it must be returned to the chamber that first introduced it. It also requires the president to provide a veto message that explains the reasons for the veto, and these remarks must be entered into the journal that Congress keeps. The Constitution specifies that the chamber that originated the legislation can take it up again and start the process of trying to override the president's veto. To successfully override a veto, both chambers must pass the legislation again with a two-thirds majority, a threshold that is usually extraordinarily difficult to reach. In most instances, when a president vetoes a bill, that will be the end of it unless political conditions change dramatically. Since 1789, only a fraction of all presidential vetoes, slightly more than 4 percent, have been overridden by Congress.

CONCLUSION

The reason why so many bills fail to make it into law is certainly no mystery. Even under the best of circumstances, the differences between the House and the Senate, along with the constitutional friction that exists between Capitol Hill and the presidency, pose many obstacles that a bill must overcome for it to become law. Added to these are the roadblocks created by how Congress goes about its legislative business. Rules and procedures followed by the two chambers at different stages in the legislative process create opportunities for lawmakers to slow down or completely stop many bills. As partisanship has increased in recent decades, the leaders and their parties tend use every opportunity presented to them to make sure that their side prevails. This has contributed to increased instances of congressional "stalemate" and a decline in legislative productivity.[12]

NOTES

1. Drew Desilver, "A Productivity Scorecard for the 115th Congress: More Laws Than Before, but Not More Substance," Pew Research Center, January 25, 2019, https://www.pewresearch.org/fact-tank/2019/01/25/a-productivity-scorecard-for-115th-congress.

2. Alexander Hamilton, *Federalist No. 70*, in *The Debate on the Constitution*, ed. Bernard Bailyn (New York: Library of America, 1993), 2:349–50.

3. This chapter's discussion of the lawmaking process was greatly aided by Walter J. Oleszek, Mark J. Oleszek, Elizabeth Rybicki, and Bill Heniff Jr., *Congressional Procedures and the Policy Process*, 10th ed. (Washington, DC: CQ Press, 2016); Donald A. Ritchie, *The U.S. Congress: A Very Short Introduction* (New York: Oxford University Press, 2016); E. Scott Adler, Jeffery A. Jenkins, and Charles R. Shipan, *The United States Congress* (New York: W. W. Norton, 2019), chap. 7; Roger Davidson, Walter J. Oleszek, Frances E. Lee, and Eric Shickler, *Congress and Its Members* (Thousand Oaks, CA: CQ Press, 2018); and Benjamin Ginsberg and Kathryn Wagner Hill, *Congress: The First Branch* (New Haven, CT: Yale University Press, 2019), chap. 5.

4. Don Wolfensberger, "Members Strain for Catchy Legislative Titles," *Roll Call*, May 28, 2010, https://www.rollcall.com/2010/05/28/members-strain-for-catchy-legislative-titles; and Philip Bump, "All the Silly Legislative Acronyms Congress Came Up with This Year," *The Atlantic*, August 2, 2013, https://www.theatlantic.com/politics/archive/2013/08/congress-acronyms-reins/312565.

5. Barbara Sinclair, *Unorthodox Lawmaking: New Legislative Processes in the U.S. Congress* (Washington, DC: CQ Press, 2012), 146–47.

6. Neil MacNeil and Richard Baker, *The American Senate: An Insider's History* (New York: Oxford University Press, 2013), 97.

7. Gregory Kroger, "The Filibuster Then and Now: Civil Rights Legislation in the 1960s and Financial Regulation," in *The U.S. Senate: From Deliberation to Dysfunction*, ed. Burdette A. Loomis (Washington, DC: CQ Press, 2012), 175.

8. Oleszek et al., *Congressional Procedures and the Policy Process*, 268.

9. Oleszek et al., *Congressional Procedures and the Policy Process*, 207.

10. Ritchie, *U.S. Congress*, 81.

11. Oleszek et al., *Congressional Procedures and the Policy Process*, 273.

12. Sarah Binder, *Stalemate: Causes and Consequences of Legislative Gridlock* (Washington, DC: Brookings Institution Press, 2003).

7

Congress and the Executive Branch

Though the framers intended for Congress to play the leading role in their new government, they took steps to keep Congress from abusing its powers. When the framers drafted the Constitution, they specifically prohibited Congress from doing things like passing bills of attainder and ex post facto laws, and they later added a Bill of Rights to the Constitution that imposed additional guardrails on Congress's power. They also divided the legislature into two chambers so that it would not act too quickly and without adequate deliberation. Finally, and most importantly, the framers incorporated in the government a complex arrangement of checks and balances to make it hard for Congress to overstep its authority.

A key component of the system of checks and balances for restraining congressional power is the president's constitutional relationship with the legislative branch. As discussed in chapter 1, the framers assigned Congress a broad range of significant powers. Yet while they certainly expected that these powers would make Congress the driving force within the system, the framers also wanted the president to be able to restrain it. They thus assigned the president a legislative role. They expected presidents to use their legislative powers, like the veto, to slow things down and even prevent bad bills from making their way into law. As they saw it, Congress would be the new government's "motor" while the president provided the "brake." Today that relationship has, for the most part, flipped. Most Americans, including politicians themselves, see the president as the one who drives change and Congress as the institution that slows things down, shifts directions from where the president wants to go, and even blocks action from taking place.[1]

Though the roles of Congress and of the president have evolved over time in response to changes on the larger political landscape, with the president emerging as a more dominant force, relations between the two have generally involved pitched battles and conflict. These sorts of struggles are a natural result of the framers' decision to give each branch the authority to act on the same set of affairs. So while Congress has most of the country's legislative power, for instance, the president has the veto power. Similarly, while presidents have the power to nominate individuals to serve in high-level executive branch positions, the Senate has the power to reject those nominees. This intermingling of powers requires both branches to "share the responsibilities of governing," and since they each represent different constituencies and are on different electoral timetables, they predictably often have different ideas about what the government should do.[2]

The history of congressional-presidential relations is filled with examples of each branch deploying its constitutional powers in pursuit of its understanding of the national interest. This sort of friction can exasperate executive and legislative officials and frustrate the American people. Yet this sort of abrasive interaction is a natural byproduct of their constitutional design.

CONGRESS, THE PRESIDENT, AND THE LEGISLATIVE PROCESS

In finalizing their decisions on the executive branch's role in the legislative process, the framers assigned to the president several responsibilities. Article II, Section 3, of the Constitution gives the president the power to convene Congress (either both chambers or just one body on its own), as well as the power to adjourn it if the two chambers cannot agree on when to end their session. Today, with both chambers meeting through the course of the year instead of just a few months at a time, as they did for about the first century and a half of the nation's existence, presidents no longer need to call Congress back into session. The last president to convene a special session was Harry S. Truman in 1948. Meanwhile, even though the Constitution authorizes the president to adjourn Congress under certain conditions, no president has ever done it, though some presidents have occasionally threatened to do so. Of greater importance are the president's powers to present Congress ideas for it to act on, to sign or veto bills Congress passes, and to implement the laws agreed to by both branches.

The President's Agenda

Article III, Section 2, of the Constitution authorizes the president to, "from time to time," provide "Congress Information of the State of the Union; and recommend to their Consideration such Measures as he shall judge necessary and expedient." When they inserted this provision in the Constitution, the framers did not intend for the president to be a major source of legislative proposals. They had a more modest view of what the president would do. And this held true through much of the American republic's first century. Certain presidents would occasionally bring some issue or legislative ideas to the attention of Congress and try, by working through members of their administrations or selected representatives and senators, to nudge it into action, but that was usually more the exception than the rule.

Even a strong president like Abraham Lincoln, who in his role as commander in chief during the Civil War dramatically expanded the powers of his office, generally steered clear of trying to direct or shape congressional decisions on domestic policies not directly related to the war effort. Neither of the two congressional parties, Democrats or Republicans, were inclined to take directions on legislative actions or priorities from the president or other members of the executive branch. Presidents understood that attitude, and they let Congress take the lead.

This state of affairs began to change, however, as the national government started to grapple with social and economic transformations unleashed by urbanization, industrialization, and the settlement of the West. Beginning with Grover Cleveland and William McKinley, presidents gradually started to flex their political muscle in dealing with Congress. Some of their immediate successors, such as Theodore Roosevelt and Woodrow Wilson, continued to expand the president's legislative role. They developed and pushed through Congress a series of progressive reforms that increased the capacity of the central government to address problems presented by the rise of large corporations, the emergence of unions, urbanization, and growing economic inequalities. Their presidencies marked the beginnings of stronger presidential leadership of Congress.[3]

Roosevelt and Wilson showed in the opening years of the twentieth century what presidents could achieve by using their powers to set the congressional agenda. Nearly two decades after Wilson's presidency, President Franklin Delano Roosevelt, also known as FDR, followed their lead. Within a few months after taking the oath of office in the spring of 1933, in fact, he had even overshadowed their accomplishments. Elected in the midst of the Great Depression, Roosevelt succeeded a president, Herbert Hoover, who had not been inclined to use his powers to advance policies to address the nation's high levels of unemployment and massive social dislocation. Roosevelt took the opposite view—and he thus brought significant and long-term change to presidential-congressional relations. His administration quickly developed and pushed through Congress several monumental pieces of legislation. These laws formed the centerpiece of the New Deal, the set of programs that established the nation's social welfare state. Roosevelt's legislative actions set the standard for what is now expected of our presidents. To this very day, presidents are tentatively evaluated based on their legislative accomplishments during their first one hundred days in office, the same number of days it took FDR to get Congress to enact his first New Deal initiatives.[4]

Because of FDR's transformational time in office, perceptions of the president's role changed, as did the presidency itself. The president is now viewed as the nation's "chief legislator," and occupants of the office have gained increased staff support to help them provide Congress with a set of legislative initiatives on a wide range of matters.

To say that the president sets the congressional agenda is not to say that lawmakers themselves do not come up with ideas for legislation, however. Legislative measures come from a wide range of people, including senators and representatives. Still, in those instances involving significant policy changes, today's legislators routinely rely on the executive to provide them with a legislative blueprint of what the president wants before they will move forward with a bill in Congress. Indeed, it is not uncommon to hear lawmakers say they are waiting on the president to get them a bill on some policy issue or another so that they can begin their work. Presidents who fail to comply with these expectations receive a great deal of criticism— from the press, the public, and even lawmakers themselves. Representatives and senators no longer complain, as their predecessors once did, that presidential legislative proposals constitute an intrusion on the Congress's constitutional responsibilities. They often want presidents to concentrate their attention on a few key issues they can address in a single legislative session, and presidents are judged by their ability to do that and succeed in translating their preferences into law.[5]

Yet presidents cannot compel lawmakers to act on their initiatives. Congress does have an important say as to what happens. It can choose to change, block, and even ignore the president's legislative priorities. Only Congress can legislate and provide funding for what the government does. To succeed in their legislative role, presidents must also be able to get the members of the two chambers to agree to pass a bill that can be sent to the White House for approval.

Working with Congress to Advance an Agenda

The president's legislative role goes beyond submitting policy initiatives to Congress and then waiting for representatives and senators to send them a bill to sign. The president and members of the administration, including White House staffers, intervene at selected stages of the legislative process, at which points they try to shape lawmakers' decisions and prod them to act to produce the legislative outcomes they are after. But presidents often find Capitol Hill studded with many minefields that can detonate and blow apart their plans. It is true that the two branches can, during times of crisis, work together and get things done quickly. In 2020, for instance, within a matter of a few weeks, the president and Congress agreed on several bipartisan bills that provided more than $3 trillion in relief to businesses, workers, schools, hospitals, and others during the early months of the COVID-19 pandemic. Yet apart from urgent matters, rapid agreement between the nation's lawmakers and the president sitting at the other end of Pennsylvania Avenue, the famous street that links the White House and the Capitol building, is rare. Many major presidential initiatives covering such important issues as immigration, energy, climate change, health care, and Social Security have been stopped or dramatically modified by lawmakers in recent years.

Presidents try to advance their initiatives through negotiations with lawmakers. A prime example of a president who was successful at this was President Lyndon Baines Johnson. Johnson pursued a sweeping legislative agenda during the mid-1960s that rivaled in scope what Roosevelt had accomplished with his New Deal. Johnson's legislative success expanded civil rights protections and created social welfare programs such as Medicaid and Medicare, which provided greater access to health care for the poor and the aged. It also included many programs to expand opportunities for children, the poor, and minorities.

Many scholars and journalists note that Johnson was successful in these efforts because of his skill in bargaining with members of Congress. Having served on the Hill in both chambers prior to his presidency—including stints leading Democrats both when they were in the minority and the majority in the Senate—Johnson knew how Congress worked and knew how to persuade its members to follow his lead. He closely followed events on the Hill and remained in near-constant contact with key legislators during pivotal points of the legislative process. He routinely called members or had them over to the White House. As he spoke with them, he vowed to use his powers to reward them for their support. He also threatened to punish them by withholding support for—or even opposing—their pet projects if they failed to support his legislative measures. Johnson's ability and willingness to work closely with all members of Congress, including Republicans, enabled him to build bipartisan coalitions and pass legislation on enormously controversial measures, such as the Civil Rights Act of 1964 and the Voting Rights Act of 1965.[6]

Yet there are limits to what presidents can accomplish through personal negotiations. A lot depends on the two sides' perceptions. When presidents are popular with the public, it is harder for members of Congress to say no. Many of Johnson's successes, for example, came early in his tenure, in the immediate aftermath of the assassination of President John F. Kennedy in 1963 and on the heels of his overwhelming landslide victory in the 1964 election. Johnson's high popularity with the American public in his early weeks and months in the Oval Office (a time sometimes known as the "honeymoon period" of a presidency) increased his stature in his dealings on the Hill. But after his popularity started to decline, even President Johnson discovered that his political skills were no match for a Congress that did not want to go along.

Lawmakers and presidents also perceive issues and problems differently, and this creates tension between them. Senators and representatives know that it is the folks back home who elect them, and that if they want to be reelected, they need to keep them happy. They are therefore inclined to focus on the specific issues and problems confronting the states and districts that sent them to Congress. They also assess and make decisions on policy issues based on how well it helps their own voters. Presidents, on the other hand, are elected by and responsive to a broader constituency. They are thus more inclined to look at how their initiatives affect national affairs as opposed to the more specific needs or interests of districts or states that lawmakers represent. In addition, presidents in their second term, because they are limited by the Twenty-Second Amendment and cannot run for the office again, often focus on policies that will secure their historical legacy, and these may be at odds with lawmakers' more immediate electoral interests.[7]

The partisan lens through which the two sides view issues and programs also shapes presidential-congressional relations. Presidents get greater support for their initiatives from their own party's lawmakers. Since parties have become more internally united and polarized, this is even more the case today than it was in the past. Lyndon Johnson could build bipartisan coalitions when he was in the White House, because congressional parties were less polarized then, making it easier for him to persuade some lawmakers on the other side of the aisle to support some items on his legislative agenda. Today, presidents rely on and get greater support for their initiatives from their own party, but they also get much less support from their partisan opponents. As a result, a president's legislative priorities typically fare better under unified government, a condition that exists when one party controls both ends of Pennsylvania Avenue. The opposite is also true. In the past, when control was divided between the parties, a condition known as divided government, presidents still managed to reach agreements with Congress on some rather significant policies. This is no longer the case, for contemporary presidents face nearly insurmountable hurdles in getting congressional support for their measures when different parties control the legislative branch.[8]

Saying No to Affect Outcomes

From the framers' perspective, the president's principal legislative role was to stop bad bills. While they gave presidents the power to block bills from becoming law, however, they also gave Congress the authority to override a presidential veto if it could muster a supermajority, or two-thirds vote. Early presidents used their veto power sparingly, only striking down legislation sent to them if they felt that it violated the Constitution. This did not change until Democrat Andrew Jackson's presidency from 1829 to 1837. Jackson believed he could strike down bills because he disagreed with the policies they contained. This touched off a major battle with Jackson's congressional opponents, the Whigs. Eventually, with the demise of the Whigs, the opposition to the president's broader use of the veto power faded away, and presidents started to enlist it more often when they disagreed with Congress.[9]

In one sense, the president's veto power is a potent weapon that can be deployed to stop Congress. Vetoes are rarely overridden. This is because of the high threshold that is required in Congress, one that is even harder to reach in today's environment because of the sharp divisions between the parties and the strong support presidents receive from their partisan colleagues on the Hill. In another sense, it is a blunt instrument, since presidents do not have the power to exercise a "line-item veto," which is a power that many state governors possess. A line-item veto enables an executive to veto, or strike out, a specific provision in a bill and allow the rest of the measure to become law. When presidents object to a provision in a bill, however, they must veto the entire bill or sign it and live with the provision they do not support.

As the years have passed, presidents from both parties have asked Congress to give them a way to exercise a line-item veto. In 1995, a Republican-controlled Congress passed legislation that gave the president authority to control expenditures by striking out certain provisions in the Balanced Budget Act of 1997. This form of the line-item veto was quickly challenged in the courts after President William J. Clinton used it to selectively strike some of the provisions in the Act. The City of New York, some medical organizations, and a farmer's cooperative impacted by the president's action all argued that the veto power as described in Article 1, Section 2, Paragraph 2, of the Constitution prohibited this sort of veto. The Supreme Court agreed, and in the case *Clinton v. City of New York* (1998), it struck down the line-item veto as unconstitutional.

Though the authority to veto only the whole bill provides a blunt instrument, presidents can deftly wield it to shape legislation more to their liking. As many political scientists note, presidents use this authority strategically as they negotiate with lawmakers. For example, they frequently threaten to veto a measure unless Congress modifies its position to accommodate the White House's preferred policy outcomes. Of course, this is not a one-way street. Congress also has some leverage that it can use to get its way in its dealings with presidents. It can insert provisions on policy that it wants but that the president opposes into a bill the president otherwise wants to sign. This strategy forces presidents to choose between either accepting the provisions they do not want or not getting any of the bill at all.[10]

Taking the Fight Outside

Presidents also try to shape outcomes on the Hill by taking their case to the American people. Political scientists call this strategy "going public."[11] Presidents as far back as Teddy Roosevelt and Woodrow Wilson in the first two decades of the twentieth century have tried to shape public opinion and thereby build support for their positions on the Hill. Those presidents and some of their immediate successors occasionally took their case to the American people. FDR, for example, regularly broadcast remarks, which came to be known as "fireside chats," to a national radio audience. "Going public" did not become a routine strategy, however, until Ronald Reagan assumed the mantle of the presidency. Reagan regularly took his case directly to the American people, encouraging them to contact and pressure their representatives and senators to support his policy initiatives.

Reagan's initial success established a precedent for later presidents. Today most presidents try to gain victories on Capitol Hill by building public support for their policy initiatives. Presidents accomplish this by coupling personal negotiations with lawmakers together with publicity blitzes that aim to shape popular sentiment in support of their programs. The White House knows that members of Congress are sensitive to the shifting currents of public opinion because of their electoral concerns. Presidents expect that once they get the public on their side, it will be easier to convince representatives and senators to support their legislative initiatives.

This presidential strategy of speaking directly to the American people, though common, is not always fruitful. Many scholars even believe that, at best, it can have only a limited impact. First, given the current polarization of the electorate, it is not easy for presidents to change the public's views on issues. Second, many lawmakers, especially in the House, come from districts that are politically lopsided, one way or the other. Third, the changing media environment makes it difficult for presidents to reach the kind of audiences they got in the past. When Reagan was president, he could command a large share of the public's attention because people had fewer media options. There were only a handful of networks, CNN was just a fledgling news outlet, and political talk radio shows were still on the horizon. There was no Internet. There were no social media platforms. Presidents of that era could, for instance, use a State of the Union address to highlight their legislative initiatives, and because that address would be carried on all the television networks that existed at the time, it would attract a sizable audience. Pretty much anyone who watched television, which at the time was one of the few in-home sources of entertainment available to people, would end up catching at least part of their address. That is no longer the case. Today, people have other, alternative sources of entertainment, from the Internet to hundreds of television channels that just keep showing their regular programming. Contemporary Americans can easily avoid the State of the Union address if they wish to do so.

Presidents also find that in this new media environment, with many more news platforms available to the public, they no longer have the public stage to themselves. In recent years, members of Congress and the parties to which they belong have followed the president's lead in trying to shape popular sentiment by mounting their own publicity campaigns. Frequently, presidents find that the opposition party will counter and thus neutralize their efforts to shape public opinion. As a result, the ability of current presidents to move popular sentiment in ways that support their policy positions is greatly constrained—though that has not kept them from trying.[12]

GOING ALONE

Given challenges they encounter in getting Congress to accept their initiatives, presidents have increasingly turned to their constitutional authority as the head of the executive branch to go around Congress and shape policy on their own. Article II, Section 1, says that "the Executive Power shall be vested in a President of the United States of America," and Article II, Section 3, holds that the president "shall take care that the Laws be faithfully executed." Article II also requires presidents to take an oath or affirmation promising to "faithfully execute" their office and to "preserve, protect and defend the Constitution of the United States."

When Congress passes legislation, it delegates power to the executive branch and its head, the president, to put the law into effect. The executive branch then figures out the details as to how that is to be done. Frequently, presidents will use their executive power to shape the implementation of a law to obtain outcomes they want.[13]

One such strategy is to use a "signing statement" to signal how the president intends to implement a law that Congress has passed. When presidents sign legislation into law, they usually issue a statement about the bill. While many of these "signing statements" are purely symbolic, presidents occasionally use them to register their unhappiness or dissatisfaction with a specific provision in the bill that they sign into law. They usually provide a constitutional reason to support their views. Frequently, they contend that the provision they object to in some way intrudes on their executive authority or constitutional role as commander in chief. In their statements, they will say they will either not enforce that part of bill or will enforce it only in a way that they believe fits with their constitutional responsibilities and oath of office.

Another way that presidents can shape outcomes is by issuing some sort of presidential directive to a part of the executive branch they lead. One of the most well-known or common directives is an executive order. Another one is a presidential memorandum. Though technically different, both direct a governmental department or agency that implements the laws that Congress enacts to undertake those responsibilities in a certain way. Both types of directives also have the force of law. Presidents have used both to make many sweeping policy changes. Presidents have used them to reorganize parts of the federal government, create new executive branch agencies, desegregate the armed services, and send federal troops to the South to oversee the desegregation of public schools. They have used them to change environmental regulations and shape policies on health care, trade, tariffs, and immigration. President Donald J. Trump used them to move forward on building a wall on the border between the United States and Mexico as well as to impose restrictions on individuals traveling to the United States from other countries during the early months of the 2020 COVID-19 pandemic. Presidents have been able to do all these things without having to rely directly on Congress.

Congress, of course, can always pass legislation overturning a president's action, but given the president's veto power and the supermajority needed in Congress to override it, that is not an easy thing for it to do. When other presidents come into office, they can also issue executive orders changing what previous presidents had done on their watch. President Trump, for example, issued an executive order in his first year in office that curbed regulations on carbon emissions by coal plants that had been put into place by an executive order signed by his predecessor, President Barack Obama. Thus, while this type of executive action provides presidents with ways of getting around Congress, its long-term impact and duration are much less certain than the policy changes that come through the legislative process.

Through presidents sometimes try to get around Congress by acting alone, Congress has an array of powers that it can use to control presidential initiatives. Some of these go beyond enacting laws and trying to overcome a presidential veto. Congress also engages in oversight of the executive branch. This involves monitoring and investigating the details of executive branch work, including how it spends its money and implements laws. Congress can use its oversight powers to call executive branch officials to testify in committee hearings about how they are carrying out their work. This enables Congress to gather information and put pressure on the administration. Because Congress controls funding, it can always cut or threaten to shrink the budget of an agency or a department if it disagrees with how the president is overseeing the implementation of a law. The Senate can signal its displeasure of presidential behavior by refusing to confirm individuals the White House wants to fill key executive branch policy positions. There are thus a variety of ways the legislature can push back against presidents who enact policies unilaterally.

Yet even though Congress does have leverage, there are practical limits to what it can do. It has limited time and resources to carry out oversight. The size of the executive branch and the complexity of the specialized work that it performs require Congress to be selective in what it investigates and monitors. Lawmakers also depend on the executive branch for much of the information they need as they push forward with their oversight activities. While Congress does have staff to help it, it is no match for the highly specialized bureaucrats working in the executive branch. Congress also controls the federal purse, but there are practical limits to the funding cuts it can make. Many constituents and pressure groups that support members of Congress rely on government programs, so cutting those funds can put representatives and senators at electoral risk. Presidents can also make recess or temporary appointments to fill vacancies in executive branch positions that otherwise require senatorial approval in the confirmation process. So while Congress can respond to the president's efforts to act alone, it must be selective in its response.

CONGRESS, THE PRESIDENT, AND FOREIGN POLICY

Just as the Constitution gives each branch a hand in shaping domestic policies, it similarly distributes the government's foreign policy powers between two of them. It assigns both the executive and the legislative branch a set of responsibilities that fall within the sphere of foreign affairs.

Article I gives Congress the authority to regulate foreign commerce between nations, the power to tax and spend; the power to raise and support an army and a navy; the power to "call forth," organize, arm, and regulate a militia; and, of course, the power to fund the military. It also gives Congress the sole authority to declare war.

While Congress has a formidable set of foreign and national security powers, Article II makes the president the civilian head of the military and the militia. It also authorizes presidents to receive ambassadors and other foreign ministers. In addition, the Constitution assigns to both branches certain tasks that are related to foreign policy. It authorizes the president, "with the Advice and Consent of the Senate, to make Treaties, provided two thirds of the Senators present concur," and to make ambassadorial, ministerial and consular appointments, subject to approval by the Senate.

Even though the framers allocated these responsibilities to the two different branches to prevent either one from getting too much leverage and control, presidents have managed to gain the upper hand. Much of this happened over the course of the twentieth century, though presidential efforts to tip the balance in their favor has longer historical roots. The extent of their success can be seen by looking at the status of relations between two sides when it comes to shaping and controlling the nation's foreign policy and providing for its security.

The contest between presidents and Congress to shape foreign policy goes all the way back to George Washington's presidency. Washington defended the powers of his office when it came to foreign affairs and thus established important precedents. Supported by arguments advanced by his secretary of state, Alexander Hamilton, Washington asserted the power of the president to define foreign policy in declaring that the United States would remain neutral in the conflict between Great Britain and France. After a brief conflict with the Senate, Washington asserted the power of a president to negotiate treaties and only submit them to the Senate for approval when the negotiations between the sides were finished. Furthermore, he sent foreign emissaries abroad without congressional approval and asserted the power to withhold information from Congress used in the negotiation of treaties.

Presidents have continued to follow Washington's lead and asserted their power to chart out the nation's foreign policy. This has been especially true since the end of World War II. Presidents have asserted control and developed the United States' stance in its relations with the rest of the world, often acting unilaterally without first seeking approval from Congress. While earlier presidents such as James Monroe and Teddy Roosevelt had done this as well, presidents since Harry S. Truman have consistently developed foreign policy doctrines that guide the United States' relations with the rest of the world. Some of those before the 1990s focused on containing communist expansion and aggression. A few, such as the administration of President Jimmy Carter, put human rights at the center of the nation's foreign policy. Recent presidential doctrines addressed new challenges presented by the rise of terrorism and the fraying of post–World War II international security structures. In his foreign policy doctrine, President George W. Bush asserted that the United States would launch preemptive strikes against terrorists or nations harboring terrorists that threatened the United States' interests. His successor, President Obama, changed course when he announced a foreign policy doctrine that promised a multilateral approach to resolving foreign policy problems.

Presidents have also unilaterally ended or pulled out of treaties negotiated by their predecessors. Carter ended a treaty to provide protection to Taiwan shortly after the United States formally established diplomatic relations with the People's Republic of China. More recently, President George W. Bush withdrew the United States from the Anti-Ballistic Missile Treaty with Russia, and President Trump pulled the country out of two agreements with Russia, the Open Skies Treaty and the Intermediate Range Nuclear Forces Treaty, that had imposed restraints on global armaments.

Congress does push back, sometimes more aggressively than at other times, and moves to assert some control over foreign policy. This is especially true when Congress is not controlled by the president's own party. Members of Congress have occasionally put enough pressure on the White House to change the president's foreign policy positions. They have, for example, persuaded presidents to support democratic movements in the Philippines. They have also used their leverage on trade policy to get the administration to support human rights movements in the old Soviet Union and China. Congress has used its power of the purse to tie the president's hands on distributing aid and military assistance to other countries as well. In recent years, Congress has imposed, over presidential objections, restrictions on funds flowing to certain governments or political movements because of concerns about human rights abuses within the country receiving the assistance. President Obama, for instance, was frustrated when the Congress withheld aid to Egypt until its government demonstrated what Congress understood to be credible progress toward restoring democratic governance. Congress has also used its oversight power to investigate and put pressure on the executive because of its foreign-policy-branch decisions.

The Senate uses its power to confirm political appointments to the executive branch as another means of checking the administration's foreign policy. Occasionally the Senate refuses to accept a nominee for a post because of concerns about the nominee's foreign policy perspective. President Clinton, for example, had to withdraw one of his nominees to lead the Central Intelligence Agency because key senators raised concerns about the nominee's political activities and policy views.

The Senate also wields its power over treaties to shape foreign policy outcomes. For example, the Senate has forced presidents to make concessions on treaties submitted to it for approval and has even gotten some presidents to pull treaties from the chamber before a vote could be taken. Senators have carried their fights on treaties to the courts as well. Some lawmakers, for example, mounted a court challenge to President Carter's decision to end a treaty guaranteeing Taiwan's security. Senators have even killed some treaties. Their chamber, for instance, dealt a significant blow to President Woodrow Wilson's effort to bring the United States into the League of Nations after World War I, when it defeated the multilateral Treaty of Versailles he negotiated. More recently, the Senate voted down an international agreement on testing nuclear weapons negotiated and submitted by President Clinton, and it failed to ratify a United Nations treaty protecting the rights of individuals with disabilities negotiated by President George W. Bush and eventually submitted to the Senate by President Obama.

Still, presidents retain the upper hand in many of these clashes, in part because it is hard for members of Congress to speak with one voice on many of these issues. The body's 535 members (435 in the House and 100 in the Senate) collectively represent too many diverse interests to allow for that kind of unanimity. Furthermore, the fact that many foreign policy issues cut across the jurisdiction of multiple committees means that usually there are too many legislative actors with too many contending positions to develop a single position. Today's deep partisan divide also limit's Congress's ability to shape foreign affairs. The position that many representatives and senators take on a president's international agenda is determined more by the party to which they belong than by the merits of the decisions themselves. Another barrier that makes it difficult for Congress to take a leading role in international policy is that most Americans are not that interested in foreign affairs. Moreover, when the legislators tangle with presidents on these matters, the latter typically have far more staff and informational resources at their disposal. As a result of all this, the usual practice is for Congress to husband its resources and political capital and exert itself on a relatively small number of foreign issues.

Finally, as is the case with domestic affairs, presidents have ways of getting around Congress by acting on their own. An example of this is a president's use of executive agreements. Executive agreements are like treaties. They are pacts entered into by the president with heads of other governments. They are binding and have the force of law. But unlike treaties, executive agreements do not require senatorial approval. As a result, presidents have turned to these more often in recent years to avoid having to make concessions to Congress or even risk outright defeat. President Obama, for instance, used executive agreements to cooperate with other countries to address the problems of climate change and the expansion of Iran's nuclear capabilities. He did that at least in part because he knew he would not get congressional approval for those actions from Republicans that controlled both houses of Congress. Of course, while presidents can bypass Congress by using executive agreements, their successors can easily get out of them. When Trump followed Obama into the White House, he canceled both deals.

CONGRESS, THE PRESIDENT, AND NATIONAL SECURITY

When the framers drafted the Constitution, they established the president as commander in chief of the nation's military, but they gave Congress the power to declare war. The framers allocated responsibilities this way to prevent the abuse of power by either branch of the government. They thought that if presidents could take the nation to war on their own, they would abuse that power, as most monarchs had done in the past. But the framers also wanted to ensure civilian control of the military and to give the country the leeway it needed to respond militarily to surprise attacks. The framers recognized that Congress would not always be in session and able to act, so they left the president enough discretion to respond to such emergencies.

While the framers sought a balance between the two branches, over time presidents have expanded their control over national security issues. As a single individual, it is relatively easy for a president to take the sort of quick, decisive action that military emergencies sometimes require. At the end of World War II, the United States assumed a leadership position in an increasingly interconnected world where nations opposed to American interests had nuclear weapons. For the first time in its history, following this war, the country established a permanent, peacetime military apparatus capable of deploying anywhere on the planet in a short period of time. As the term "Cold War" implies, from 1945 until the early 1990s, the United States was prepared to go to war on a moment's notice. It was as if the country was in a permanent emergency situation. The perceived threats posed by "rogue nations" and terrorism have led the country to stay on this wartime footing even beyond the fall of the Soviet Union, its primary geopolitical rival for much of the second half of the twentieth century. Presidents point to this picture of a dangerous international environment, and to their Article II constitutional powers, to defend their dominant position in national security matters.[14]

In the initial years following the adoption of the Constitution, the two branches were more evenly matched in their efforts to control defense policy. President Washington stood firm and asserted the power to declare the nation's neutrality in the war between Great Britain and France, but he also worked closely with Congress when he sent troops to secure the nation's western border. Many presidents who followed stuck to Washington's precedent. While President Thomas Jefferson took a more active role by using military forces to protect United States' shipping interests from acts of piracy, he also courted Congress to get support for his action. In many instances in these early decades, it was Congress, not the president, that supported a more aggressive national defense policy. It was the more nationalistic "war hawks" in Congress—leading figures such as Henry Clay from Kentucky and John C. Calhoun from South Carolina—who took a hard-line stance against Great Britain and eventually succeeded in getting James Madison to request a congressional declaration of war. This was the first time Congress used that power, and it marked the official start of the War of 1812.

Later presidents seized the initiative on national security policy. President James Polk provoked conflict with Mexico to expand the territory of the United States and, in 1846, managed to get Congress to again declare war for only the second time in its history. During the Civil War, President Abraham Lincoln expanded presidential power to deal with the southern states who had seceded from the Union. Lincoln invoked his constitutional powers and oath of office to justify such actions as seizing private property, expanding the military, shutting down courts, and mounting a naval blockade on southern states. President Lincoln later took care to ask Congress to authorize his actions, but these mid-nineteenth-century events nonetheless established a precedent of Congress deferring to a president in times of crisis. This pattern recurred on several occasions, including during World War I and World War II. After declaring war in both instances, Congress enacted legislation that delegated to presidents a vast array of important powers to be used both at home and abroad. These laws authorized presidents to take many actions to regulate and control the nation's economy to support the war effort, and so they further expanded the White House's influence over domestic affairs.

After World War I, Congress reclaimed much of the power it had given to President Wilson. Things were different after World War II. The Cold War between the United States and communist countries, and especially the Soviet Union, transformed the postwar environment for both the president and Congress. Because of the Cold War, the United States' interests in the world expanded to include many nations who were aligned with it in the fight against communist expansionism. The world also became a more dangerous place, driven in part by technological changes that ushered in a new generation of fearsome weaponry. Congress lacked both the capacity to respond quickly and decisively to threats, both at home and abroad, presented by new and potentially devastating weapons of war as well as by the ability to move troops swiftly. To protect the United States and its more extensive interests abroad, and to do so with the energy and speed it required, Congress gave the president more authority to act. It also provided the president with more administrative resources and a sizable standing military and intelligence network to command. Presidents applied these resources to contain communist expansionism, and Congress generally complied.[15]

By the mid-1960s, however, the relationship between the branches had become more contentious. The United States' military intervention in Vietnam, authorized by Congress in the 1964 Gulf of Tonkin Resolution, took center stage in American politics, as the conflict continued to expand to include countries like Laos and Cambodia. Steps taken by Presidents Lyndon B. Johnson and Richard M. Nixon to increase the United States' involvement in the Vietnam War eventually produced significant civil unrest in the states. As popular support for the war declined, Congress struggled to pressure the president to get the United States out of the war and bring the troops back home. Lawmakers also took action to limit a president's unilateral ability to commit troops abroad. Aiming to prevent another Vietnam from happening again, they passed the War Powers Act of 1973. This legislation, passed over President Nixon's veto, put restrictions on a president's ability to commit troops abroad, and it imposed a time limit for how long the president could keep them there if Congress did not authorize the action.

Despite the support it received from lawmakers, the War Powers Act has had only a minimal effect on restraining the president. Since its enactment, presidents have on many different occasions sent troops into harm's way. This has prompted many scholars to conclude that the legislation has been more symbolic than substantive and that presidents, once again, have managed to tip the balance of power in their favor.

Congress, meanwhile, has ceded power to the president on a number of important national security fronts. In the wake of the al-Qaeda terrorist attack on the World Trade Center in New York on September 11, 2001, President George W. Bush sought—and Congress quickly provided— sweeping authorization to use military force to invade Afghanistan to eliminate terrorist camps within its borders. The Bush administration also sought and received from Congress the authority to launch a preemptive war against Iraq, arguing that its leader, Saddam Hussein, harbored in his country weapons of mass destruction that posed a danger to the United

States. The claims that Iraq possessed weapons of mass destruction eventually proved false. Nonetheless, the United States maintained a troop presence in both Afghanistan and Iraq for many years afterward, and both Obama and Trump have used that authority to combat terrorism to launch attacks or air strikes against terrorist targets in countries like Syria, Libya, Yemen, Somalia, and Pakistan.

As is the case with foreign policy, Congress has ample authority to restrain presidents. It can check presidents through oversight and funding of the military and through the Senate's power to confirm executive branch political appointees. But this is usually difficult for it to do, because when troops are stationed abroad in dangerous settings, it is politically hard for Congress to cut military expenditures. Members of Congress are reluctant to leave themselves vulnerable to accusations that they are not being supportive of U.S. troops. In addition, the public frequently supports a president's use of force in times of crisis, at least initially, and this makes it difficult for many members of Congress to stand up to the executive branch in the early days of an emerging military crisis. Finally, as is the case with foreign policy, members of Congress have fewer incentives to concentrate on monitoring the executive branch's national security initiatives. Presidents hold a privileged position in guiding the activities that intelligence and national defense agencies engage in as those bodies gather, interpret, and control the information necessary to make decisions on national security policy. So while Congress can hold investigative hearings and receive intelligence briefings from various executive agencies, it is often difficult for it to compel the president to share all relevant information.

CONGRESS AND PRESIDENTIAL IMPEACHMENT

While the framers of the Constitution thought that Congress would be the "motor" of the American political system and that the president would provide the "brake," they had enough foresight to recognize there might be occasions when executives would become too overbearing and abuse their powers. As a result, they gave Congress authority, under certain circumstances, to remove presidents and others in the executive branch as well as members of the judiciary who violated the public trust. That process is impeachment.[16]

The Constitution spells out the workings of the impeachment process. Article I, Section 2, says that the House of Representatives has the "sole Power of Impeachment." This applies to the president, vice president, and other executive branch officers as well as to members of the federal judiciary. This means that it is the job of the House to bring the charges against the official or judge. Article I, Section 3, gives the Senate "the sole Power to try all Impeachments." It also stipulates that in those cases when the "President of the United States is tried, the Chief Justice shall preside" and says that conviction by the Senate in an impeachment trial requires a supermajority of "two thirds of the Members present." The Constitution specifies conditions for impeaching and removing a president, a vice president, and executive officers in Article II, Section 4. That list includes acts of "Treason, Bribery, or other high Crimes and Misdemeanors."

Impeaching and removing judges and executive branch officials, including presidents, is an extreme course of action. Only three presidents in American history—Andrew Johnson, Bill Clinton, and Donald Trump—have been impeached by the House of Representatives. None of them was convicted and removed from office by the Senate. While President Trump was impeached twice, the Senate did not take up any action on his second impeachment until his term of office ended and Joseph R. Biden assumed the presidency. Thus, Trump was no longer president when the Senate received the second articles of impeachment from the House. One president, Richard Nixon, resigned from office before the full House voted on articles of impeachment charging him with criminal wrongdoing and abuse of power.

Some judges have been removed from their positions through impeachment, but all executive branch officials, including the three presidents and one cabinet member (Secretary of War William K. Belknap, from the Grant administration), who have been impeached have been acquitted by the Senate. This is because removal from office requires meeting a high bar. While impeachment needs only a majority vote in the House, the two-thirds vote required for conviction in the Senate ensures that it will usually be difficult to remove an official and especially the president, the country's duly elected chief executive. In all three instances involving the impeachment of a president, the Senate vote fell short of the necessary two-thirds vote. The Senate came close to the two-thirds vote needed to convict a sitting president only once, when its members acquitted Andrew Johnson by a single vote. The vote was more evenly divided in the other two cases. In all three cases combined, only a single senator of the president's own political party voted to convict and remove the president. The senator was Willard Mitt Romney, a Republican from Utah who had been his party's presidential nominee in 2012. Romney voted to convict President Trump on one of the two charges brought to the Republican-controlled Senate by the Democratic majority party in the House.

As the history of presidential impeachment suggests, it is a process in which political calculations and considerations play a very significant role. As long as the parties are internally united and polarized—and have significant representation in Washington—it is highly unlikely that impeachment will result in a successful conviction and removal from office. Clearly that is something the framers anticipated and, as the threshold they established for removal suggests, something that they preferred. The framers did not want impeachment to be used as a routine congressional procedure to oust a president whom lawmakers did not like or with whom they disagreed. Instead, the framers intended that impeachment be a tool that Congress could use to protect the nation from presidents who flagrantly abused executive power, violated their oath of office and the public trust, and posed a danger to the core values of a democratic government.

CONCLUSION

While the framers of the Constitution set up Congress to be their new government's driving force, they took precautions to make sure that it would not abuse its authority. Toward that end, they required Congress to share governing responsibilities with others. They believed that this would make it difficult for Congress to gain too much power.

At the heart of this system in which different institutions share governing responsibilities is the relationship between Congress and the president. While the framers expected that the legislative body, because of its powers and its relationship to the citizenry, would be the driving force in the political system, they anticipated that the president would serve to moderate and check its excesses. Over time this relationship has changed. In the legislative process, the president is now the leading actor on the nation's political stage. Today's Congress frequently plays the role of slowing down and obstructing presidential initiatives, prompting presidents to go around Congress and advance their policy preferences by acting on their own.

As presidents have taken on an increased role in shaping domestic policy, they have also expanded their power over Congress in shaping foreign and defense policies. Some of this shift in power is because of the constitutional authority of the presidency, which in today's world gives presidents an advantage over Congress. Some of the expanded power is the result of the greater resources and specialized information that are available to each president. But some of this change has been brought on by Congress itself. Confronted with a more dynamic and complex international environment, Congress has ceded to the executive more power to determine the country's relations with the rest of the world and provide for its security.

NOTES

1. Richard J. Ellis, *The Development of the American Presidency*, 3rd ed. (New York: Routledge Press, 2018), 142–43.

2. Matthew J. Dickinson, "The President and Congress," in *The Presidency and the Political System*, 11th ed., ed. Michael Nelson (Thousand Oaks, CA: CQ Press, 2018), 408.

3. Ellis, *Development of the American Presidency*, 166–80.

4. Ellis, *Development of the American Presidency*, 180.

5. Ellis, *Development of the American Presidency*, 186.

6. Edward J. Berkowitz, "The Great Society," in *The American Congress: The Building of Democracy*, ed. Julian E. Zelizer (New York: Houghton Mifflin, 2004), 566–83.

7. Roger H. Davidson, Walter J. Oleszek, Frances E. Lee, and Eric Schickler, *Congress and Its Members*, 16th ed. (Thousand Oaks, CA: CQ Press, 2018), 312–17; and Benjamin Ginsberg, *Presidential Government* (New Haven, CT: Yale University Press, 2016), 198–200.

8. E. Scott Adler, Jeffery A. Jenkins, and Charles R. Shipan, *The United States Congress* (New York: W. W. Norton, 2019), 330–33. For a discussion of legislative productivity under conditions of divided government in an earlier era, see David R. Mayhew, *Divided We Govern: Party Control, Lawmaking and Investigations, 1946–2002*, 2nd ed. (New Haven, CT: Yale University Press, 2005).

9. For this change in perspective on using the veto, see Ellis, *Development of the American Presidency*, 160–66.

10. Adler, Jenkins, and Shipan, *United States Congress*, 316.

11. Samuel Kernell, *Going Public: New Strategies of Presidential Leadership* (Washington, DC: CQ Press, 1997). For a discussion of the evolution of this strategy, see Ellis, *Development of the American Presidency*, 103–28.

12. For a discussion of challenges presidents face in moving public opinion, see George C. Edwards, *On Deaf Ears: The Limits of the Bully Pulpit* (New Haven, CT: Yale University Press, 2003). Matthew A. Baum and Samuel Kernell discuss the initial changes cable news brought to the media environment and the challenges presidents confronted in getting out their message in this setting in "Has Cable Ended the Golden Age of Presidential Television?," *American Political Science Review* 93 (March 1999): 99–114, https://www.cambridge.org/core/journals/american-political-science-review/article/has-cable-ended-the-golden-age-of-presidential-television/3DAA130F7715665639D20C2D9EA8A2BD. On the development of congressional communication campaigns to respond to presidents "going public," see Gary Lee Malecha and Daniel J. Reagan, *The Public Congress: Congressional Deliberation in a New Media Age* (London: Routledge Press, 2012).

13. The discussion of presidential strategy of trying to govern alone is based on the discussion provided by Andrew Rudalevige, "The Presidency and Unilateral Power: A Taxonomy," in *The Presidency and the Political System*, 11th ed., ed. Michael Nelson (Thousand Oaks, CA: CQ Press, 2018), chap. 17.

14. The following discussion on the evolution of the relationship between the executive and legislative branches in making national security policy is based on

Ellis, *Development of the American Presidency*, chap. 5, and Ginsberg, *Presidential Government*, chap. 9.

15. Ginsberg, *Presidential Government*, chap. 9; and Benjamin Ginsberg and Kathryn Wagner Hill, *Congress: The First Branch* (New Haven, CT: Yale University Press, 2019), chap. 7.

16. For a discussion of impeachment, see Ellis, *Development of the American Presidency*, 534–36; and Michael Nelson, "'The Firing, Retiring, and Expiring of Presidents': Impeachment, Disability, Resignation, and Death—from the Constitution Convention to Donald Trump," in *The Presidency and the Political System*, 11th ed., ed. Michael Nelson (Thousand Oaks, CA: CQ Press, 2018), 548–56.

8

Congress and the Judiciary

A common view of the relationship between Congress and the federal judiciary is that Congress makes laws and federal courts review them and determine if they are constitutional. This view portrays justices as disinterested in the outcome of the social and political struggles that produce the laws they review. It sees them as arbiters whose only concern is that the other parts of the government play by the Constitution's rules. Supreme Court Chief Justice John Roberts gave voice to this vision in his opening statement to the Senate Judiciary Committee during his 2005 confirmation hearing. "Judges are like umpires," he told the senators. "Umpires don't make the rules; they apply them." He promised that, if confirmed, "I will remember that it's my job to call balls and strikes and not to pitch or bat."[1]

While this portrayal contains some truths, many scholars, like Louis Fisher, claim that it is unrealistic to compare judicial review to umpires just calling balls and strikes. Fisher, a longtime student of our system's separation of powers, notes that umpires have an objective standard they use to call balls and strikes: "A strike zone (which) is the width of the plate and a height between a batter's knees and shoulders." Fisher asks, "What is the strike zone for such constitutional values as due process, equal protection, free speech, religious liberty, and cruel and unusual punishment?" He notes that many of the Constitution's most important passages are genuinely ambiguous and can reasonably be interpreted quite differently by constitutional experts as well as by citizens. Fisher concludes that judges thus inevitably make policy decisions when they interpret the constitutionality of congressional policy decisions. As he puts it, "In applying law, judges inevitably make law."[2]

In this chapter, we will see that Congress's interactions with the judiciary, much like its relations with the presidency, frequently involve a struggle. This is because, as Fisher indicates, the line between making law and interpreting law is not as clear as many, including several justices who sit on the bench, surmise. When they review the actions of the other branches, judges necessarily and unavoidably touch on matters that are also in the executive's and legislature's domains, and individuals serving in those two branches regularly feel that the court has overstepped its bounds. As we explained in chapter 1, the framers of the Constitution intentionally created three branches of government that shared some powers, in the hope that this power-sharing arrangement would encourage each branch to keep a watchful eye on the others. So this sort of struggle and disagreement is how the system was intended to work.

Yet interactions between Congress and the courts are also shaped by the more episodic forces that sometimes sweep through the American political landscape. These include things like the changing ideological complexion of parties, the growth of presidential power, and fundamental economic changes. The struggles, sometimes violent ones, that occasionally flare up around cultural and social issues also impact congressional-judicial relations. The contests over slavery; the rights to form unions, to vote, and to marry; and the disagreements about the role of religion in public life and public demonstrations against police brutality—these sorts of experiences also leave their mark on interbranch relations.

Exploring the interactions of Congress and the courts reveals both how difficult it is to disentangle policy making from constitutional interpretation and how the absence of a clear line separating those two activities results in conflict between our government's branches. Just as the Constitution and historical experiences lead the legislative and executive branches into each other's affairs and create conflict, so, too, are the legislative and judicial branches prone to engage in each other's business in ways that heighten tension between them.

THE CONSTITUTIONAL FOUNDATION

Article III of the Constitution begins by declaring, "The judicial Power of the United States, shall be vested in one supreme Court, and in such inferior Courts as the Congress may from time to time ordain and establish." Its next sentence gives the individuals who serve on these courts a lifetime appointment—they can serve so long as they exhibit "good behavior"—and assures that their salaries cannot be reduced during their time on the bench. These provisions establish the judiciary as an independent and coequal branch of government. While the Constitution's language does not explicitly give the judicial branch the power to be the sole arbiter or interpreter of the Constitution, Article VI gives courts the power to uphold the central government's laws and treaties as the "supreme Law of the Land."

This original arrangement reflects the aspirations and conflicts that led to the Constitution's adoption. You will recall from chapter 1 that Americans agreed the Articles of Confederation needed to be reformed. Beyond that, though, they disagreed about the kinds of reforms that would best serve the country. As we discussed, the federalists thought that the Articles' main drawback was that it did not sufficiently empower the national government to secure goals that most Americans desired. These included things like fending off European powers, providing for a safe western expansion, and creating an economic setting that would encourage wealthy foreigners to invest in American enterprises eager to develop the country's many natural resources. Their opponents, the antifederalists, feared a strong national government. They thought it was not democratic enough, and they felt that states, where the government was closer to the people, were better suited to protecting peoples' rights and liberties.

Article III's opening sentences give voice to both sides' perspectives. On the one hand, it makes the Supreme Court a federal institution that has the authority to shape law. Moreover, once they take their place on the federal bench, the Constitution encourages these justices to serve their country in ways that they think best, even if they disagree with the decisions made by the president, Congress, or the states. It does this by assuring judges that they cannot lose their jobs or have their salaries cut by these other elected officials who might be angry with their rulings.

On the other hand, the Constitution gives Congress, which represents and is responsive to both states and citizens, the power to create other federal judicial tribunals and to set the size of the Supreme Court and determine the types of cases that can be appealed to it. Most of the federal court system is, therefore, in the hands of the people's elected representatives. Congress also has some leverage over who can sit on the federal bench. To become an Article III judge, an individual must be nominated by the president and confirmed by the Senate, thereby giving states a say in who gets to sit on these courts. Recall that under the original constitution, senators were elected by state legislatures and that presidents were elected by the Electoral College, whereby each state was given a direct voice.

One issue the Constitution does not clearly establish is where exactly the legislative and judicial powers begin and end, since Congress makes policy and the Court reviews whether such policies are constitutionally sanctioned. Today, many believe that the Supreme Court has the final say on what the Constitution means, and indeed some justices have made this claim. The term *judicial supremacy* is sometimes used to describe this idea of the Court's role. But there is a countervailing view, called departmentalism, that, while not as widely supported as it was in the founding era, has always maintained that all three branches have the power and the duty to interpret the Constitution in the performance of their public duties. Supporters of this view remind us that before they assume their offices, members of Congress and the president are required to take an oath promising to uphold the Constitution. Accordingly, "as public officials sworn to uphold the Constitution, senators and representatives have an independent duty to interpret it." Under this view, the other branches are obliged to obey a particular court ruling in a narrow sense, as it applies to the specific facts of a single case, but they are not required to abide by the Court's interpretation when dealing with similar situations in the future.[3]

BUILDING THE FEDERAL JUDICIARY

To get the new government off the ground, the first Congress passed the Federal Judiciary Act of 1789. It determined that the Supreme Court would have a chief justice and five associate justices. It also established a three-tiered court system. It created three U.S. Circuit Courts below the Supreme Court. Their main role was to be the federal system's principal trial courts. Below them were district courts, established in each state and presided over by a federal judge with the power to hear cases involving admiralty and maritime law and other minor matters.

This legislation also assigned two Supreme Court justices to each of the three circuits, who, together with local federal judges, oversaw trials within their assigned circuit. The justices began to complain almost immediately that the extensive travel this required, called "circuit riding," was so grueling that it imperiled their health. They also pointed out that since the circuit cases they oversaw might lead to appeals they would review at the Supreme Court, their participation in these trials could create an appearance of impropriety that would undermine public confidence in the judiciary.

This issue got swept into the United States' great partisan battle that broke out between the Federalists and Jefferson's Democratic-Republicans, the nation's first political parties, and it led to one of the most important Supreme Court cases in history. John Adams, a leading Federalist, lost the presidency to Thomas Jefferson in the election of 1800. As Adams's term was ending, he and the Federalist-dominated Congress rushed to reorganize the judiciary by creating three more circuits and adding sixteen new justices to serve in them, thereby relieving Supreme Court justices of their circuit-riding responsibilities. They also quickly named a political opponent of Jefferson's, John Marshall, as chief justice. This Federalist effort to reorganize the Court was literally the final act of Adams's presidency—he was still at his desk at 9:00 p.m. on his last day in office, trying desperately to fill as many judicial posts as he could.[4] Jefferson's supporters criticized this as a last-minute partisan move to put the judiciary in Federalists' hands. Referring to Adams's fevered effort to fill the slots before he left DC, they branded these new justices as "midnight judges." When Jefferson took over the presidency, some of the new judges, though they had been confirmed by the Senate, had not yet received their official appointment or commission, so he ordered his secretary of state, James Madison, not to deliver them. One of those who did not receive his commission was William Marbury, and he sued the administration, asking the Supreme Court to order Madison to deliver his commission.

In *Marbury v. Madison*, a unanimous Court noted that normally it would be illegal to withhold Marbury's commission, but it also declared that the section of the 1789 Judiciary Act that gave the Supreme Court jurisdiction in this case was an unconstitutional expansion of its authority. As such, since it did not have the authority to rule on this case, the Supreme Court could not order Madison to deliver the commission. As an important aside, the Court claimed in *Marbury* that it had the power of judicial review, which is the power to declare null and void any law or action that it understood to be unconstitutional. Even though, as we noted earlier, the Constitution does not explicitly give the Court this power, ever since *Marbury* most Americans have accepted the federal courts' authority to overturn laws and policies made by the other two branches and state and local policy-making bodies.

Meanwhile, the new Jeffersonian-dominated Congress kept the six circuit courts created by the previous Congress but abolished the sixteen judge positions that had been created to run them, which meant that Supreme Court justices resumed their circuit-riding duties. Those justices continued to ride their circuits in one form or another until 1891, when Congress passed the Evarts Act and did away with that requirement. This set the stage for eliminating circuit courts in 1911, when Congress reorganized the heart of the Article III court system and created the one that exists today. It is still a three-tiered system, with U.S. circuit courts of appeal directly below the Supreme Court, and with U.S. federal district courts below them. Now most trials begin in district courts, and participants are guaranteed the right to appeal those rulings to the circuit court level if they disagree with the district court's decision. While cases can be appealed from circuit courts to the Supreme Court, that court is under no obligation to grant those appeals a hearing.

OTHER "INFERIOR" COURTS

Other congressional additions to the federal judiciary also reflect larger forces and controversies that historically drive American politics. In the late 1800s, industrialization led to a more globalized American economy. This divided the Democrats and Republicans on the issue of using tariffs to manage the importation of goods. In 1890, to relieve the burden that both customs and tariff disputes placed on federal courts, Congress created the Board of General Appraisers. Then in 1909, Congress created the U.S. Customs Appeals Court to hear appeals from that board. As the number and complexity of controversies that came to it increased, Congress changed the board to the U.S. Customs Court and made it part of the judicial branch. In 1980, Congress reorganized this body yet again, and it is now the U.S. Court of International Trade.

Congress sometimes creates new judicial bodies to respond to emergencies. In 1942, just as the country was emerging from the Great Depression and World War II was in its early stages, a new concern appeared on the horizon. Many feared that during this rapid and sometimes chaotic economic transformation, prices of essential civilian goods and war materials would skyrocket. Congress passed the Emergency Price Control Act, which created an Office of Price Administration (OPA) to impose regulations to deter price gouging and undue profiteering. The OPA put price ceilings on rents and on products such as gas, oil, sugar, coffee, and meats and even rationed some of these products. Congress also created an Emergency Court of Appeals to adjudicate those who wanted to appeal OPA's regulatory decisions. Congress abolished this court in 1962.

In the early 1970s, the country was in a deep recession, due in part to the Vietnam War, an emerging gasoline energy crisis, and a dangerously high inflation rate. President Richard M. Nixon, nearing the middle of his first term, supported passage of the Economic Stabilization Act of 1970, which put government controls on wages, salaries, rents, interest rates, dividends, and the price of some goods. This measure generated discontent. Some individuals and businesses charged that these regulations were unconstitutional infringements on their economic freedom. Congress created the Temporary Emergency Court of Appeals to rule on appeals raised by such disgruntled parties. The legislation that created this court initially expired in 1974. But Congress, responding to popular pressure, renewed it and expanded the Court's jurisdiction several times until it was disbanded in 1992.

Congress created another new judicial body in the 1970s as it responded to a different kind of emergency. In our chapter on congressional committees, we discussed the House's and Senate's investigations into the Nixon White House's criminal conduct during the 1972 presidential campaign.

That congressional oversight revealed that for several years, U.S. intelligence agencies had unlawfully spied on American citizens. To prevent such illegal activity while still granting intelligence agencies the secrecy they need to conduct their mission, Congress in 1978 passed the Foreign Intelligence Surveillance Act. In part, this act created the Foreign Intelligence Surveillance Court, often referred to by the act's acronym as the FISA Court. It is currently composed of eleven U.S. district court judges who are appointed by the Supreme Court's chief justice. When intelligence agencies believe that they have reason to suspect that a U.S. citizen may be conspiring with a foreign entity against American interests, they must go before the FISA Court and, in a hearing that is closed to the public, present their evidence, and solicit the Court's permission to conduct their surveillance. The FISA Court represents Congress's attempt to strike a balance between giving intelligence agencies the power they need to protect the country from spies while at the same time protecting those citizens' rights that national security policies are supposed to preserve. The FISA Court has always generated controversy. Some think it impairs the government's ability to defend against foreign aggression, while others believe it puts American freedoms at risk. A recent example of this controversy was the concern that some Trump administration officials had about the FISA Court's role in the government's investigation of the relationship between some Trump campaign officials and Russian agents.[5]

CONTESTED TERRAIN: THE SIZE OF THE SUPREME COURT AND THE DESIGN OF THE JUDICIAL BRANCH

Congress exercised its power to set the size of the Supreme Court on seven different occasions in the country's first 80 years but has refrained from doing so in the subsequent 151 years. Congress established a six-member Supreme Court shortly after it first convened. It added a seventh seat in 1807, and in 1837 it added two more justices and created two more circuit courts. In both instances, Congress was responding to the growing size of the country as new states joined the union.

The forces that threatened to tear the country apart before the Civil War generated a flurry of congressional alterations, both to the size of the Supreme Court and to the design of the circuit courts. In 1862, to limit the influence of southern states, Congress rearranged circuit courts to reduce from five to three the number of circuits composed entirely of slave states. This allowed President Abraham Lincoln to nominate more northerners to circuit court positions. The next year, Congress created a tenth U.S. circuit court and added a tenth seat to the Supreme Court, further aligning the judiciary with northern perspectives. Right after the Civil War, in 1866,

Congress again readjusted the circuit courts so that only two were composed of former slave states, allowing for yet another expansion of northern federal judges. In that same year, fearing that President Andrew Johnson was not sufficiently dedicated to supporting the freedoms of former slaves, Congress reduced the size of the Supreme Court from ten to seven, thus denying the president the chance to nominate someone to that high court. In 1869, when President Ulysses S. Grant entered the White House, Congress increased the size of the Supreme Court to nine. Congress has since left the size of the Supreme Court intact and has not engaged in any large-scale alteration of the other Article III courts.

The fact that Congress has not formally exercised these powers since 1869 may obscure how its capacity to do so has continued to shape congressional-judicial relations. In the late 1880s and early 1900s, progressives in state legislatures and their allies in Congress passed laws to attack the glaring inequalities caused by a largely unregulated economy. But a conservative Supreme Court held firm and overturned many of those initiatives. In *Lochner v. New York* (1905), a case that defines that Supreme Court era of resistance to economic reform, the Court struck down a law that protected workers. The law it overturned made it illegal to require a baker to work more than ten hours a day or more than sixty hours per week. Claiming that this violated what they called a "liberty of contract," the Court declared the legislation unconstitutional. This "Lochner-era" Court regularly sided with big business. As one scholar notes, "during one stretch from 1887 to 1905, the court heard 16 cases involving railroads, and ruled for the railroad companies in 15 of them."[6] This outraged progressives, who called for reforms like abolishing the power of judicial review and adding more seats to the Supreme Court.

Progressives' demands for such reforms helped lay the groundwork for an even more decisive effort to redesign the Court: President Franklin Delano Roosevelt's 1937 "court-packing" plan. After winning a landslide reelection to a second term with large Democratic majorities in both houses of Congress, President Roosevelt (FDR) and his legislative allies were eager to expand their efforts to reinvigorate an economy still mired in an economic depression. FDR had promised to provide the American people a "new deal" when he was first elected in 1932. But the Supreme Court had blocked his efforts by declaring many of his initiatives to be unconstitutional. A frustrated FDR responded by proposing to expand the number of seats on the Supreme Court for each justice over the age of seventy, limiting the number of such additional seats to six. While some argued that this would help make justices' workload more manageable, the real intent was to create a Supreme Court majority that would uphold the president's New Deal programs. In one sense, the president's plan backfired. With many Americans objecting to what they understood to be an attack on the judicial branch's independence, Congress defeated the plan. FDR's plan to "pack" the Court also affected his future relations with Congress, since it helped turn many southern Democrats who opposed the plan against some of FDR's other more progressive initiatives. Yet not long after the president's proposal to expand the Court, one of its members, Justice Owen Roberts, changed the way he often voted, and in the famous 1937 *West Coast Hotel v. Parrish* case, upheld the constitutionality of minimum-wage laws. Subsequent Court rulings upheld other New Deal policies. There are good reasons to believe that Justice Roberts did not simply cave to the very real pressure applied by FDR's plan to get Congress to pack the Court, but his altered voting pattern is commonly referred to as "the switch in time that saved nine."

More recently, some who opposed President Trump and the conservative direction of the Republican Party called on Democrats to again consider expanding the Supreme Court's size. Representative Ro Khanna, a Democrat from California and a member of the House Progressive Coalition, pointed out that the Supreme Court was hearing far fewer cases than it had heard in the 1980s and suggested that adding more justices would increase its productivity. Another liberal activist said that there was "nothing magical about the number nine" and observed that "nine is not some sort of global norm. The U.K.'s Supreme Court consists of 12 justices. Israel's has 15." Instead of calling it "court packing," this activist called it "court balancing," and he urged Democrats, if they reclaimed control of the Senate and won the White House, to "add at least two new seats to the Supreme Court and fill them with left-wing, well qualified women of color." Other changes have also been suggested. Representative Khanna, for instance, says that "there is no reason to have lifetime tenure on the Supreme Court." He argues that Congress does not need a constitutional amendment to limit service on that Court to a specified number of years. In his view, the constitutional provision that protects the careers of federal judges so long as they exhibit good behavior is not undermined if a judge is moved from one federal court to another. He suggests moving Supreme Court justices to U.S. circuit courts of appeals once they hit the limit that he hopes Congress will place on Supreme Court service.[7]

CONTESTED TERRAIN: IMPEACHMENT

Impeachment is another constitutional feature that shapes congressional-judicial relations. Recall that Article II says, "The President, Vice President and all civil Officers of the United States, shall be removed from Office on Impeachment for, and Conviction of, Treason, Bribery, or other high Crimes and Misdemeanors." Members of the judiciary are included in the "all civil Officers of the United States" language. The impeachment mechanism works the same as it does when Congress considers removing a president. A simple majority of House members is needed to draft articles of impeachment that specify the charges against a judge, and then the Senate holds a trial based on those charges. Conviction and removal from office requires a supermajority or two-thirds vote in the Senate.

This is a powerful weapon to aim at the Court. But it is rarely used. Fifteen federal judges have been impeached by the House, leading to eight convictions and four acquittals in the Senate. Three impeached justices resigned from the bench before their Senate trials were completed. The first impeachment occurred in 1803, when a district judge was convicted and removed from his post a year later. Given that he was widely perceived as mentally unstable and was frequently intoxicated during his court's proceedings, the outcome was not entirely unexpected. This initial experience proved to be indicative of the sorts of behavior that tend to lead to Senate convictions. All eight judges removed from office through impeachment had engaged in behavior that most would agree made them unfit to serve on the bench.

The outcome of the second Senate trial and the only Supreme Court justice to be impeached set another important precedent. It pretty much established that federal judges should not be removed from office if their only offense is to rule in ways that conflict with the president's or Congress's policy goals. Supreme Court Justice Samuel Chase, a staunch Federalist with "a volcanic personality," made clear just how much he opposed Jefferson and his party in the hotly contested 1800 election. When Jefferson and his party gained power in 1800, the House voted to impeach Justice Chase on eight charges. The last article accused him of using his position to promote his political goals, "tending to prostitute the high judicial character with which he was invested, to the low purpose of an electioneering partisan."[8] Chase certainly was not shy about expressing his opinions. Even Chief Justice John Marshall, a Federalist colleague, admitted at the Senate trial that Justice Chase's behavior on the bench could be "tyrannical, oppressive, and overbearing."[9] Yet even in this highly charged partisan environment, after reviewing the behavior of an overbearing and contentious character that was easy to dislike, six senators from Jefferson's party found him not guilty on all counts, and the Senate was unable to muster the supermajority it needed to remove him from the Supreme Court.

Yet the long-standing tradition of the elected branches choosing to withhold their impeachment and conviction power when they have a policy disagreement with the Court could change. Throughout time, many individual members of Congress have talked about impeaching federal judges even though the legislature usually resists these calls to action. Future president Gerald Ford, when he was a House member in 1970, talked of starting impeachment proceedings against Supreme Court Justice William Douglas for, among other things, writing a short book that

Ford described as articulating "a fuzzy harangue evidently intended to give historic legitimacy to the militant hippie-yippie movement."[10] In more recent years, at the state level, there have been calls to impeach state judges who have dealt with issues that touch party divides—for instance, justices who have ordered state legislators to redraw district boundaries or who have ruled on marriage rights for same-sex couples.[11] The United States today is witnessing bitter partisan battles over a host of issues that rival earlier conflicts. As parties vie for power, these battles have the potential to express themselves in congressional-judicial clashes. Indeed, there was some congressional talk of impeaching Justice Brett Kavanaugh even before he completed his first term on the Court, as a reaction to his bitter Senate confirmation hearing, which divided the American people.[12]

CONTESTED TERRAIN: SUPREME COURT NOMINATIONS

The way partisan battles impact relations between Congress and the courts is perhaps nowhere more evident than in Senate judicial nomination hearings, especially when there is a vacancy on the Supreme Court. From one perspective, this is what might be called a high constitutional moment. The president nominates an individual for the Senate's consideration of that person's fitness to serve on the highest court in the land. Originally, federal judicial nominations were taken up on the Senate floor, and while parts of its deliberations were leaked to the press, that debate was not open to the public. The practice of the Senate holding committee hearings to discharge its confirmation responsibilities did not start until 1916, when President Woodrow Wilson nominated Louis Brandeis to the Supreme Court. This was a controversial nomination, in part because Brandeis was the first Jewish person ever to be nominated and anti-Semitism was rampant in the United States. Brandeis was also perceived as willing to take on corporate interests in the middle of the Court's Lochner era. The first nominee ever to show up in person at a Senate judicial nomination hearing was Felix Frankfurter in 1939. Twenty years later, Justice Potter Stewart's experience before the Senate Judiciary Committee in 1959 began to resemble the kind of hearing that we are familiar with today, where the nominees engage in some lengthy verbal give-and-take with committee members.

Judicial nominations have continued to evolve since then, though the causes of some of these more recent changes have historical roots that extend all the way back to the 1913 ratification of the Seventeenth Amendment, which led to the popular election of senators. As the government took on more responsibility over economic affairs during the second half of the twentieth century, it also started to grapple with social and cultural issues like segregation, voting rights, abortion, gender and racial inequalities, and the role of religion in public affairs. Much of this happened during the middle of the Cold War, from 1945 through 1991, which put national security policy front and center and increased presidential power. These developments increased senators' incentives to expand their own activities, if for no other reason than to remain competitive in their next election by currying favor with interests affected by these changes. The rise of television provided senators with another incentive to be more aggressive in judicial confirmation hearings, which became a platform for them to appease voters back home and even advance their own careers within the chamber. Some even dreamed of using exposure gained through these hearings to launch a bid for the White House. The government's expanded policy roles also put the Court front and center, as it was asked to review the constitutional status of many controversial initiatives. And all of this unfolded just as the two parties started sorting themselves out ideologically, with liberals moving to the Democratic Party and conservatives gathering in the Republican camp.

In 1987, the confluence of these forces created a highly visible and bruising battle between a Democrat-controlled Senate and a Republican president, when Ronald Reagan nominated Robert Bork to fill a seat on the Supreme Court. Bork had a long and very public career as an academic. He had also served in the Nixon administration and as a judge on the U.S. Court of Appeals for the District of Columbia. He had taken many positions on a range of issues and was a leading thinker in conservative legal circles. Many interest groups lined up to testify both for and against his nomination. Some of those opposed to his elevation to the Supreme Court created a sophisticated publicity campaign that portrayed him as a radical conservative who wanted to reverse many of the recent Court's decisions that supported civil and reproductive rights. The Senate finally denied Bork a seat on the high court, angering many of his supporters who charged that his opponents misrepresented his positions and maligned his character. Indeed, since then, when people think that an individual has been treated unfairly in the confirmation process, they often say that the person was "borked."

This 1987 experience started a new chapter in how the Senate handles its nomination responsibilities. Today's hearings are now highly publicized partisan fights. The whole process now takes longer, involves more interest groups, and attracts more media attention, as senators, presidents, and parties use these hearings as opportunities to portray themselves favorably to their supporters and to raise money for their own political campaigns.

Senate procedures have also changed since then. Traditionally, individual senators had the power to filibuster a nominee they opposed. But as the partisan stakes surrounding judicial decisions increased, the willingness of majority parties to extend this privilege to their colleagues in the minority decreased. In 2005, Senate Majority Leader Bill Frist, a Republican from Tennessee, threatened to eliminate the filibustering of judicial nominees altogether. Many considered this move drastic and even referred to it as "the nuclear option." In response, a bipartisan group of senators, known as the "Gang of Fourteen," devised a compromise that temporarily convinced the majority party not to trigger the "nuclear option." But the pressure pushing against bipartisan cooperation continued to build, and eight years later, in 2013, a Democratic Senate deployed that option. In a close 52–48 vote, with three Democrats joining all the Republicans in opposition, it eliminated the use of filibusters on all executive nominees requiring Senate confirmation, except for those nominated to the Supreme Court.

In 2016, a Republican Senate majority further exacerbated the partisan tensions surrounding the Court when it refused to hold a hearing on President Barack Obama's Supreme Court nominee, Merrick Garland. Nominated in March of a presidential election year, Senate Majority Leader Mitch McConnell, a Republican from Kentucky, argued that the opening ought to be kept vacant to give the president elected in November the opportunity to fill the seat. Democrats were outraged that a sitting president was denied even the chance of a hearing for his nominee, leaving the Court shorthanded for about a year. It was particularly galling that a nominee such as Judge Garland was treated this way. While he certainly seemed to lean in a Democratic direction, some liberal Democrats were unhappy that Obama, a Democrat, had chosen such a moderate. Garland had served on the same appeals court as Chief Justice John Roberts for about two years, and according to one account they voted the same way about 85 percent of the time.[13] The chief justice once said that those who may have found themselves disagreeing with Merrick Garland had better reconsider their opinion. Before Obama announced Garland's nomination, Senator Orrin Hatch, a Republican from Utah, reported on a talk he had had with the president. "(Obama) told me several times he is going to nominate a moderate, but I do not believe him. He could easily name Merrick Garland, who is a fine man. He probably will not do that because this appointment is about the election. So I am pretty sure he will name someone the (liberal Democratic base) wants."[14] Despite the fact that President Obama nominated an ideologically moderate such as Garland, the Republican-controlled Senate stuck to its refusal to grant him a hearing.

Partisan wrangling over the Court flared again when Senate Republicans agreed in October 2020 to hold a hearing for Amy Coney Barrett, President Trump's nominee to the Court. One of the reasons they had cited for denying President Obama a hearing for his nominee was that the vacancy on the Court occurred too close to the next presidential election—in March 2016, eight months before the next election. When the GOP-controlled Senate moved ahead with President Trump's nominee and confirmed her to the Court eight days before the 2020 election, many Democrats were outraged. Speaking for many Democratic members of Congress, Senate Minority Leader Charles Schumer declared that "the truth is, this nomination is part of a decades-long effort to tilt the Judiciary to the far right to accomplish though the courts what the radical right and their allies, Senate Republicans, could never accomplish through Congress."[15] The final 52–48 Senate vote putting Barrett on the Court reflected this deep partisan divide. Only one Republican opposed her, and no Democrat supported her. It was the first time in 151 years that a justice was placed on the Court without even one vote from a member of the minority party.[16]

COMPLETING THE CIRCLE

Some worry that contemporary clashes between the Congress and the federal judiciary could fundamentally alter the American system of government. While Congress has long been held in low public esteem, the Supreme Court historically has been much admired by most Americans, and that admiration has been a real source of power. Recall that even though most Americans overwhelmingly supported the New Deal programs of the 1930s, citizens rallied to the Court's defense when they thought that President Roosevelt was attacking it. This is especially critical since the courts depend on the president's "power of the sword" and Congress's "power of the purse" to enforce their rulings.

Here is a dramatic example that illustrates how respect for the Court has in the past been a genuine source of real power. The Supreme Court's 1954 decision in *Brown v. Board of Education* to desegregate public schools was fiercely opposed by many people. After a federal court in 1957 ordered that nine African American students be allowed to enroll in the all-white Central High School in Little Rock, Arkansas, the governor, Orval Faubus, deployed the state National Guard and ordered it to surround the school and prevent those students from entering the building. Throngs of white citizens, some waving Confederate flags, showed up to demonstrate their support of Faubus's opposition to the Court's decree.

Initially, it was not clear what the federal government was going to do. President Dwight D. Eisenhower did not talk much about race in public and seemed to think that the courts had overstepped their bounds in some civil rights decisions. Yet he was determined to enforce the Court's decision. He sent troops from the U.S. Army's 101st Airborne Division to Little

Rock, the first time since Reconstruction that a president deployed troops to the South to compel obedience to federal law, and ordered them to see to it that those nine students could attend that school. Using his control of the sword—federal bayonets—the president made sure state officials complied with the Court's decision. He also delivered a dramatic Oval Office address to the nation to make clear that the national government would use its power to enforce Court decisions, even ones that were unpopular and openly resisted by states.[17]

Some worry that as the judiciary becomes implicated in partisan battles on the Hill, it will lose the deep respect that it has long enjoyed. Recent public opinion polls indicate that there may be reason for concern. Two surveys conducted in the summers of 2015 and 2019 track how citizens who identify as Republicans or Democrats feel about the Supreme Court. On the heels of Court decisions on the Affordable Care Act and same-sex marriage that disappointed many conservatives, only 33 percent of Republicans had a favorable view of the Supreme Court in 2015, while close to double that number, 62 percent, of Democrats did. In August 2019, after several years of the Trump presidency and the appointment of two conservative jurists to the Supreme Court, those percentages were flipped. A whopping 75 percent of Republicans reported a favorable view of the Court in 2019, compared to only 49 percent of Democrats.[18]

CONCLUSION

Though partisanship on the Hill poses a threat to the stature of the Court, we know that Congress and the courts have survived through many a tumultuous time. Past performance is no guarantee of future results, to be sure, but it does remind us that each branch has the ability to adopt and change to meet the powerful forces that occasionally threaten to tear the fabric of the country apart. Even in today's highly charged political environment, surprises are still possible, as two June 2020 court cases demonstrate. Those Supreme Court decisions involved hot-button issues that set Democrats against Republicans. One case was written by Justice Neil Gorsuch, who was nominated by President Trump and whose elevation to the Supreme Court was enthusiastically supported by many conservative senators. In his majority opinion, Justice Gorsuch disappointed many of those senators by arguing that Title VII of the 1964 Civil Rights Act protects gay and transgender employees since it prohibits job discrimination "because of sex."

The other case was written by Chief Justice Roberts, whose nomination to the high court had been opposed by many liberal senators, including then senator Obama. In his opinion, Justice Roberts rejected the Trump administration's efforts to dismantle the program President Obama put into place to protect undocumented immigrants brought to the country as children, an initiative popularly referred to as DACA. Some congressional reaction to this decision reminds us that individuals in the Congress and the judiciary regularly disagree with each other about how to distinguish policy making from constitutional interpretation. Criticizing this ruling, Senator Tom Cotton (R-AR) accused the chief justice of acting more like an elected official than a judicial one. He said that if Justice Roberts believed he had "such excellent political judgment," he ought to "travel to Iowa for the caucuses and see if he can earn the votes of his fellow Americans. If he wants to be the Chief Justice though, he should follow the law and should uphold the Constitution and our laws as they are written."[19]

No one can predict exactly how these two branches will continue to interact in the years ahead. Yet we do know that while their relationship is inextricably linked to those forces that shape the whole of the American polity, each branch has the capacity to surprise their contemporary admirers and detractors, and each has the potential to point the American people in a new direction.

NOTES

1. You can see a video clip of Justice Roberts comparing judges to umpires here: https://www.c-span.org/video/?c4505745/judge-john-roberts-opening-statement -confirmation-hearing-us-chief-justice. You can read the transcript of his confirmation hearing before the Senate Judiciary Committee, including his opening statement (which begins on page 55), here: https://www.judiciary.senate.gov/imo /media/doc/GPO-CHRG-ROBERTS.pdf.

2. Louis Fisher, *Defending Congress and the Constitution* (Lawrence: University of Kansas Press, 2011), 330.

3. Robert A. Katzmann, *Courts and Congress* (Washington, DC: Brookings Institution Press, 1997), 112; see, too, Susan R. Burgess, *Contest for Constitutional Authority: The Abortion and War Powers Debates* (Lawrence: University Press of Kansas, 1992); Keith E. Whittington, *Political Foundations of Judicial Supremacy: The Presidency, The Court, and Constitutional Leadership* (Princeton, NJ: Princeton University Press, 2007); Paul Brest, "The Conscientious Legislator's Guide to Constitutional Interpretation," *Stanford Law Review* 27, no. 3 (1975): 585–601; Abner J. Mikva, "How Well Does Congress Support and Defend the Constitution," *North Carolina Law Review* 61, no. 4 (1983): 587–611.

4. Robert V. Remini, *The House: The History of the House of Representatives* (New York: HarperCollins, 2007), 72–73.

5. Information in this and the preceding section can be found in a variety of sources, including Michael A. Bailey, Forrest Maltzman, and Charles R. Shipan, "The Amorphous Relationship between Congress and the Courts," in *The Oxford Handbook of The American Congress*, eds. Eric Schickler and Frances E. Lee (Oxford: Oxford University Press, 2013), 834–58; Patrick C. Reed, "The Origins

and Creation of the Board of General Appraisers: The 125th Anniversary of the Customs Administrative Act of 1890," *Journal of the Federal Circuit Historical Society* 11 (2017): 91–110; The Federal Judicial Center, "Timelines of the Federal Judicial History," https://www.fjc.gov/history/timeline/8276; U.S. Foreign Intelligence Surveillance Court, "About the Court," https://www.fisc.uscourts.gov/about -foreign-intelligence-surveillance-court; U.S. Office of Price Administration (1941–1947) Archives and Special Collections, Kathryn A. Martin Library, University of Minnesota, Duluth, https://libarchive.d.umn.edu/index.php?p=creators /creator&id=278; James R. Elkins. "The Temporary Emergency Court of Appeals: A Study in the Abdication of Judicial Responsibility," *Duke Law Journal* 1978 (1978): 113–53, http://lawlit.net/writings/TECA-Duke.pdf.

6. Thomas M. Keck, "The Supreme Court Justices Control Whether Court-Packing Ever Happens: They Must Give the Elected Branches Room to Address Societal Needs," *Washington Post*, November 19, 2018, https://www.washingtonpost .com/outlook/2018/11/19/supreme-court-justices-control-whether-court -packing-ever-happens.

7. See "Are The Democrats Ready To Get Radical?," *The Intercept*, October 11, 2018, https://theintercept.com/2018/10/11/deconstructed-live-special-are -democrats-ready-to-get-radical; and see Medi Hasan, "Pack the Supreme Court," *The Intercept*, September 30, 2018, https://theintercept.com/2018/09/30/pack -the-supreme-court.

8. See U.S. Senate, "Senate Prepares for an Impeachment Trial," https://www .senate.gov/artandhistory/history/minute/Senate_Tries_Justice.htm.

9. Frank Thompson Jr. and Daniel H. Pollitt, "Impeachment of Federal Judges: An Historical Overview," *North Carolina Law Review* 49, no. 1 (1970): 87, 98.

10. Thompson and Pollitt, "Impeachment of Federal Judges," 87, 90.

11. See, for instance, "2011 Year in Review: Record Number of Impeachment Attempts against Judges for Their Decisions," *Gavel to Gavel: A Review of State Legislation Affecting the Courts*, http://gaveltogavel.us/2011/12/27/2011-year-in -review-record-number-of-impeachment-attempts-against-judges-for-their -decisions/; and see Douglas Keith. "Impeachment and Removal of Judges: An Explainer," Brennan Center for Justice, March 23, 2018, https://www.brennancenter .org/our-work/analysis-opinion/impeachment-and-removal-judges-explainer.

12. Domenico Montanaro, "New Calls to Impeach Justice Kavanaugh: How It Would Work and Why It Likely Won't," *NPR*, September 16, 2019, https://www .npr.org/2019/09/16/761193794/new-calls-to-impeach-justice-kavanaugh -how-it-would-work-and-why-it-likely-wont.

13. Richard Wolf. "Merrick Garland, John Roberts Usually Agreed on Appeals Court," *USA Today*, April 6, 2016.

14. John Gizzi, "Orrin Hatch Says GOP Scotus Refusal Just 'The Chickens Coming Home to Roost,'" NewsMax, March 13, 2016.

15. Todd Ruger, "Senate Confirms Amy Coney Barrett but Controversy Follows Her to the Supreme Court," *Roll Call*, October 26, 2020.

16. Nicholas Fandos, "Senate Confirms Barrett, Delivering for Trump and Reshaping the Court," *New York Times*, October 26, 2020.

17. Picture of the crowd that gathered at Central High, https://www.youtube .com/watch?v=ym8rdtq-KBE; text of President Eisenhower's address to the nation,

https://www.eisenhowerlibrary.gov/sites/default/files/research/online-documents /civil-rights-little-rock/1957-09-24-press-release.pdf; video of President Eisenhower's address to the nation, https://www.youtube.com/watch?v=ZzT5v_ICU6I; "60 Years On, a Look Back at the Little Rock Nine," interview with Ernest Green, one of the students who integrated Little Rock's Central High School, Associated Press, September 24, 2017, https://www.youtube.com/watch?v=ym8rdtq-KBE.

18. "Negative Views of Supreme Court at Record High, Driven by Republican Dissatisfaction," Pew Research Center, July 29, 2015, https://www.people-press .org/2015/07/29/negative-views-of-supreme-court-at-record-high-driven-by -republican-dissatisfaction; Claire Brockway and Bradley Jones, "Partisan Gap Widens in Views of the Supreme Court," Pew Research Center, August 7, 2019, https://www.pewresearch.org/fact-tank/2019/08/07/partisan-gap-widens -in-views-of-the-supreme-court.

19. Julia Musto, "Sen. Tom Cotton Slams Justice Roberts on DACA Decision for Applying 'Different Standards' to Trump and Obama," Fox News, June 23, 2020, https://www.foxnews.com/media/tom-cotton-slams-chief-justice-john -roberts-daca-decision.

Conclusion

Congress is an institution that everybody loves to make jokes about or malign. As its poor showing in public opinion polls indicates, most Americans hold it in low esteem. People do not trust Congress or even like it. Its favorability ratings usually put it at the bottom of the list of American institutions. Ironically, Congress, the only branch of government that the people have a direct hand in selecting, ranks far below the judiciary, the least democratic of the three branches of government. Even the president is more popular than Congress. President Donald Trump, only the third chief executive ever to be impeached, who had some of the lowest public approval ratings ever recorded by a president, still managed to come in ahead of Congress in the polls that have been taken during his time in the Oval Office.[1]

Popular discontent with Congress is shared by many scholars and journalists. They have written book after book and article after article describing the institution's sad state. Former members of both parties have also added their voice to those disappointed by Congress. Many lawmakers now use their farewell addresses on their chambers' floors to chronicle the institution's failings and speak to its lack of civility and its unwillingness to reach compromise. They usually end their farewell by imploring their colleagues to rededicate themselves to restoring harmony and civility to the institution and to making it work for the people who sent them to office in the first place: the American citizens. Some even continue to press their case after stepping down from office. In early 2020, in an unprecedented move, a bipartisan group of seventy former senators joined to pen an open letter in the *Washington Post* lamenting the decline of the Congress. They charged it with neglecting its constitutional responsibility by ceding large swaths of power to the executive branch. The brunt of their criticism was directed at the Senate, which they portrayed as especially dysfunctional.

The general thrust of their claim is that today's senators put partisanship above all else as they wield their control of procedures to advance the interests of their parties. They concluded their open letter by urging sitting senators to create a bipartisan caucus committed to bringing consensus building and compromise back to the institution they once inhabited.[2]

CONGRESSIONAL INACTION

When given the chance, people of all political stripes and from all walks of life recite a litany of complaints about congressional performance. Right at the top of that list is congressional stalemate. They say Congress gets bogged down too easily. They bemoan its partisan bickering, gridlock, and failure to reach compromise. They believe that it does not address the problems of the day and that it does not get anything done. Many grouse that members are more interested in gaining partisan advantage than collectively acting to resolve the nation's problems.[3]

There is evidence to support all of these complaints. Today, Congress spends fewer hours in session and in legislative work than it did roughly fifty years ago. Both the House and the Senate hold far fewer committee hearings than they did back then. They are also much less productive. They pass fewer major pieces of legislation, and they also spend less time conducting oversight of executive branch activities.[4] Even when they are in the nation's capital, the need to raise campaign funds for themselves and their parties for the next cycle of elections distracts them from their legislative and oversight responsibilities. Many also spend a considerable amount of time in news stations, in front of cameras, and on social media as they make the case for their party's agenda or their own reelection. Most members also make frequent trips back to their states and districts, often flying home Thursday evening and coming back to the Hill on Monday afternoon, and in an election year they cut back their time in DC even more.

Much legislation that is introduced dies in Congress and never makes it out of committee. Only a fraction of the number of bills that are introduced in a legislative session ever get taken up for consideration. Yet even when Congress does decide to move on a bill, the chances of it making its way to the president's desk are slim. This is because of the many hurdles the bill must surmount. While it may pass the House, where a majority can more easily prevail, it is often killed in the Senate. Sometimes this is because the Senate is in the other party's hands, putting it at odds with the House majority. But even when one party controls both chambers, legislation is frequently derailed and even stopped by a Senate minority that wields its power to filibuster legislation—a strategy that it is more inclined to employ in today's partisan congressional environment.

At times, Congress's inability to act undermines its stature and even creates chaos in the lives of American citizens. Just in the last decade, policy disagreements within Congress and between it and the president resulted in three government shutdowns, one during the Obama presidency and two during the presidency of Donald Trump. This interrupted the delivery of important services the government routinely provides to U.S. citizens and led to a downgrading of the national government's credit rating.

Congress has been unable to move on other key problems important to large segments of the American population as well. These include, to name just a few, issues like immigration reform, the problem of gun violence in schools and society, climate change, access to health care, information technology's threat to privacy rights, the power of large corporations, growing social and economic inequalities, continued entanglements in wars in distant lands, and a government debt that continues to spiral.

Still, that is only part of the story. Indeed, in early 2020, Congress managed to respond quickly, and on a bipartisan basis, to the economic challenges posed by the coronavirus pandemic. In the matter of just a few weeks, it passed legislation providing almost $3 trillion of financial assistance to workers and businesses. Congress has other impressive achievements it can point to: it enacted legislation that addressed the economic and banking crisis of the Great Recession of 2008, passed laws that dramatically increased Americans' access to health insurance, and reformed and imposed regulations on the financial industry. And during the first two years of the Trump presidency, it passed sweeping legislation that changed the tax code, and it reached a bipartisan agreement with the administration on a major prison reform bill that Trump signed into law in December 2018.

The belief that the state of congressional politics today is dramatically and wholly different than in days gone by is, in part, due to a nostalgic tendency to view American political history through rose-colored glasses. As earlier chapters discussed, there were times in the past that bills routinely failed to win congressional support. In some eras, members elected to the chambers were too raucous or inebriated to get much done. They often tried to settle disputes more through violence than through calm, reasoned appeals. There were other occasions when overbearing leaders single-handedly killed legislation, as they did during the early years of the progressive reform movement. Then, through the first half of the twentieth century, the institution bottled up and routinely defeated legislation advancing civil rights for African American citizens—sometimes advancing their reasons for doing so with vicious, ugly rhetoric.

The hope that Congress will work like a well-oiled machine is also at odds with the framers' vision. They hoped that the system's friction would slow things down and prevent momentary congressional responses to fluctuations in public opinion from making their way into public policy outcomes. That is why they put Congress in a system where the different branches of government could check one another and occasionally even tie things up. That is also why they divided the institution into two chambers that would have different election cycles and represent different interests. As Benjamin Ginsberg and Kathryn Hill note, the framers "were hardly legislationists." What they meant by that is the framers did not want Congress to write a lot of complex legislation that few people would be able to understand and that would have to be frequently revised, since that would threaten to undermine the government's legitimacy. Ginsberg and Hill conclude that, when viewed from the framers' perspective, the U.S. Congress "is not exactly a broken branch."[5]

DELIBERATIVE CAPACITY

Yet while Madison and the other framers did indeed believe that Congress should not act with haste, they also expected something more from it. They wanted it to be a deliberative body. They expected that lawmakers would gather together to honestly discuss and debate the issues, offer evidence for their positions and make arguments to one another and adjust their positions in light of those arguments they considered persuasive to arrive at policy outcomes that would advance the public good.[6]

Many believe that, when judged from the perspective of promoting deliberation, today's Congress falls short of the mark. They argue that the current Congress spends too little time working through the details of legislation, and they criticize Congress for failing to provide itself with adequate staff resources to help it gather the information necessary to make many of its decisions. They also believe that in this more polarized context, members are less prone to change their views and more inclined to spend their time scoring political points than working for the common good and the general welfare of the nation. In addition, deliberation is hard to carry out in today's congressional environment, in which leaders play a greater role in driving decisions and bypassing regular procedures. Congressional leaders now circumvent committees, tinkering with the work of committees that do get assignments, and routinely shut members of the minority out of deliberations. More and more major policy decisions are made in the upper echelons of the parties, by chamber leaders in consultation with just a handful of strategically placed members.

There certainly is merit in the argument that today's Congress has a hard time living up to its role as a deliberative body. There are a great many forces and procedures that make deliberation difficult to realize. This includes those points in the legislative process where high levels of partisanship especially discourage and even shut down thoughtful discussion and debate. Still, as the discussions in this book's previous chapters make clear, there were many other occasions in the history of Congress in which the chambers were either too rowdy or too regimented by strong-arm control from the top to realize the goal the framers set for them. Even in the era before Congress became more polarized, and greater power rested with committees, many of the members found themselves often deferring to the wishes of a small and unrepresentative group of committee chairs who wielded great control within the institution, and who could punish them if they fell out of line.

CONGRESSIONAL DECLINE

Finally, as those seventy former senators indicated in their 2020 letter to the *Washington Post*, there is an uneasiness with the contemporary Congress's relations with the executive branch within a system specifically designed to check and balance power. Many believe that Congress, the first branch of government, has abdicated its role in the American political system by being too deferential to presidents, enabling them to take the initiative and even act on their own in domestic policy as well as foreign affairs. Admittedly, some only seem to regard this state of affairs as a problem when their party is not in charge of the White House, but others worry that this trend has thrown our system of government out of balance.

This is not the first time Americans have heard such concerns expressed. Nor is this the first time that presidents have wrested greater power or control from Congress. Nor is it even the first time that Congress has deferred to presidents and followed their lead. Most often this shift in the balance of power between the two branches has occurred during crisis situations like the Civil War, World War I, and the Great Depression. These crises created opportunities for presidents to expand the powers of their office. Yet in the years following these extraordinary events and challenges, Congress always managed to reassert itself. Even in the years following World War II and in the middle of the Cold War, Congress managed to reboot itself to reclaim some of the leverage it had lost to an increasingly powerful office of the president—an ascendant executive branch that the historian Arthur Schlesinger Jr. referred to as the "Imperial Presidency."[7] Less than a decade after Schlesinger coined that term in 1973 to describe the president, however, the shift in the balance of power back to Congress was noticeable enough that scholars started writing about its "resurgence."[8]

The challenge Congress faces today is thus a familiar one, even if it is also a daunting one. As presidents have expanded their powers and increasingly turned to going around the legislative branch through unilateral actions, Congress must push back if it wants to reclaim its position within the system of separation of powers and checks and balances that the framers set for it. It has done this before and, as this book has discussed, it certainly has many tools available to it to do so yet again. The dilemma it now confronts is how to manage this at a time in which Congress, like the nation it represents and reflects, is deeply divided and polarized into competing partisan camps.

NOTES

1. Jacob Jarvis, "Congress Has a Lower Approval Rating than Donald Trump: Poll," *Newsweek*, May 26, 2020, https://www.newsweek.com/donald-trump-congress-approval-ratings-monmouth-poll-1502191.

2. Justine Coleman, "Seventy Former Senators Propose Bipartisan Caucus for Incumbents," The Hill, February 25, 2020, https://thehill.com/homenews/senate/484556-70-former-senators-propose-bipartisan-caucus-of-incumbent-members.

3. "Congress and the Public," Gallup, 2016, https://news.gallup.com/poll/1600/congress-public.aspx.

4. Norman J. Ornstein, Thomas E. Mann, Michael J. Malbin, Andrew Rugg, and Raffaela Wakeman, "Vital Statistics on Congress," Brookings Institution, March 2019, https://www.brookings.edu/multi-chapter-report/vital-statistics-on-congress.

5. Benjamin Ginsberg and Kathryn Wagner Hill, *Congress: The First Branch* (New Haven, CT: Yale University Press, 2019).

6. See Joseph Bessette, *The Mild Voice of Reason: Deliberative Democracy and American National Government* (Chicago: University of Chicago Press, 1994).

7. Arthur M. Schlesinger Jr., *The Imperial Presidency* (Boston: Houghton Mifflin, 1973).

8. James L. Sundquist, *The Decline and Resurgence of Congress* (Washington, DC: Brookings Institution, 1981).

Appendix: Standing Committees of the U.S. Congress

U.S. House of Representatives	U.S. Senate
Agriculture	Agriculture, Nutrition, and Forestry
Appropriations	Appropriations
Armed Services	Armed Services
Budget	Banking, Housing, and Urban Affairs
Education and Labor	Budget
Energy and Commerce	Commerce, Science, and Transportation
Ethics	Energy and Natural Resources
Financial Services	Environment and Public Works
Foreign Affairs	Finance
Homeland Security	Foreign Relations
House Administration	Health, Education, Labor and Pensions
Judiciary	Homeland Security and Governmental Affairs
Natural Resources	Indian Affairs
Oversight and Reform	Judiciary
Rules	Rules and Administration
Science, Space and Technology	Small Business and Entrepreneurship
Small Business	Veterans' Affairs
Transportation and Infrastructure	
Veterans' Affairs	
Ways and Means	

Sources: https://www.house.gov/committees; https://www.senate.gov/committees/index.htm.

Recommended Readings

Adler, E. Scott, Jeffery Jenkins, and Charles R. Shipan. 2019. *The United States Congress.* New York: W. W. Norton.

Baker, Ross K. 1989. *House and Senate.* New York: W. W. Norton and Company.

Barrett, David M. 2005. *The CIA and Congress: The Untold Story from Truman to Kennedy.* Lawrence: University Press of Kansas.

Bessette, Joseph. 1994. *The Mild Voice of Reason: Deliberative Democracy and American National Government.* Chicago. University of Chicago Press.

Burgess, Susan R. 1992. *Contest for Constitutional Authority: The Abortion and War Powers Debates.* Lawrence: University Press of Kansas.

Caro, Robert A. 2003. *Master of the Senate: The Years of Lyndon Johnson.* New York: Vintage Books.

Caro, Robert A. 2013. *The Passage of Power: The Years of Lyndon Johnson, Volume IV.* New York: Vintage Books.

Davidson, Roger H., Susan Webb Hammond, and Raymond W. Smock, eds. 1998. *Masters of the House.* Boulder, CO: Westview Press.

Davidson, Roger H., Walter Oleszek, Frances E. Lee, and Eric Schickler. 2018. *Congress and Its Members.* 16th edition. Thousand Oaks, CA: CQ Press.

Deering, Christopher J., and Steven Smith. 1997. *Committees in Congress.* Washington, DC: CQ Press.

Dodd, Lawrence D., and Bruce I. Oppenheimer. 2016. *Congress Reconsidered.* Thousand Oaks, CA: CQ Press.

Ellis, Richard J. 2018. *The Development of the American Presidency.* 3rd edition. New York: Routledge.

Fenno, Richard B. 1973. *Congressmen in Committees.* Boston: Little, Brown.

Fenno, Richard B. 2003. *Home Style: House Members in Their Districts.* New York: Pearson.

Fiorina, Morris P. 1989. *Congress: Keystone of the Washington Establishment.* 2nd edition. New Haven, CT: Yale University Press.

Freeman, Joanne B. 2018. *The Field of Blood: Violence in Congress and the Road to Civil War.* New York: Farrar, Straus and Giroux.

Ginsberg, Benjamin, and Kathryn Wagner Hill. 2019. *Congress: The First Branch.* New Haven, CT: Yale University Press.

Jacobson, Gary. 2013. *The Politics of Congressional Elections.* New York: Pearson Longman.

Katzmann, Robert A. 1997. *Courts and Congress.* Washington, DC: Brookings Institution Press.

Kernell, Samuel. 1997. *Going Public: New Strategies of Presidential Leadership.* Washington, DC: CQ Press.

Lee, Frances E. 2016. *Insecure Majorities: Congress and the Perpetual Campaign.* Chicago: University of Chicago Press.

Loomis, Burdette A., ed. 2012. *The U.S. Senate: From Deliberation to Dysfunction.* Washington, DC: CQ Press.

Maass, Arthur. 1985. *Congress and the Common Good.* New York: Basic Books.

MacNeil, Neil, and Richard A. Baker. 2013. *The American Senate: An Insider's History.* New York: Oxford University Press.

Malecha, Gary Lee, and Daniel J. Reagan. 2012. *The Public Congress: Congressional Deliberation in a New Media Age.* New York: Routledge.

Mann, Thomas E., and Norman J. Ornstein. 2012. *It's Even Worse Than It Looks: How the American Constitutional System Collided with the New Politics of Extremism.* New York: Basic Books.

Mayhew, David R. 2004. *Congress: The Electoral Connection.* 2nd edition. New Haven, CT: Yale University Press.

Mayhew, David R. 2005. *Divided We Govern: Party Control, Lawmaking, and Investigations, 1946–2002.* New Haven, CT: Yale University Press.

Miller, William Lee. 1998. *Arguing about Slavery: John Quincy Adams and the Great Battle in the United States Congress.* New York: Vintage Books.

Oleszek, Walter J., Mark J. Oleszek, Elizabeth Rybicki, and Bill Heniff Jr. 2016. *Congressional Procedures and the Policy Process.* Washington, DC: CQ Press.

Peters, Ronald M., Jr. 1997. *The American Speakership: The Office in Historical Perspective.* 2nd edition. Baltimore, MD: Johns Hopkins University Press.

Polsby, Nelson W. 2004. *How Congress Evolves: Social Bases of Institutional Change.* New York: Oxford University Press.

Quirk, Paul J., and Sarah A. Binder, eds. 2005. *The Legislative Branch.* New York: Oxford University Press.

Remini, Robert V. 2007. *The House: The History of the House of Representatives.* New York: HarperCollins.

Ritchie, Donald A. 2016. *The U.S. Congress: A Very Short Introduction.* 2nd edition. New York: Oxford University Press.

Rohde, David W. 1991. *Parties and Leaders in the Postreform House.* Chicago: University of Chicago Press.

Schickler, Eric. 2001. *Disjointed Pluralism: Institutional Innovation and the Development of the U.S. Congress.* Princeton, NJ: Princeton University Press.

Sinclair, Barbara. 1995. *Legislator, Leaders, and Lawmaking: The U.S. House of Representatives in the Postreform Era.* Baltimore, MD: Johns Hopkins University Press.

Sinclair, Barbara. 1989. *The Transformation of the U.S. Senate.* Baltimore, MD. Johns Hopkins University Press.

Sinclair, Barbara. 2012. *Unorthodox Lawmaking: New Legislative Processes in the U.S. Congress.* Washington, DC: CQ Press.

Smith, Steven S. 2014. *The Senate Syndrome: The Evolution of Procedural Warfare in the Modern U.S. Senate.* Norman: University of Oklahoma Press.

Strahan, Randall. 2007. *Leading Representatives: The Agency of Leaders in the Politics of the U.S. House.* Baltimore, MD: Johns Hopkins University Press.

Theriault, Sean M. 2013. *The Gingrich Senators: The Roots of Partisan Warfare in Congress.* New York: Oxford University Press.

Wilson, Woodrow. 1981. *Congressional Government.* Reprint of 1985 edition. Baltimore, MD: Johns Hopkins University Press.

Young, James Sterling. 1966. *The Washington Community, 1800–1828.* New York: Harcourt Brace Jovanovich.

Zelizer, Julian E. 2004a. *The American Congress: The Building of Democracy.* New York: Houghton Mifflin.

Zelizer, Julian E. 2004b. *On Capitol Hill: The Struggle to Reform Congress and Its Consequences, 1948–2000.* Cambridge: Cambridge University Press.

Zelizer, Julian E. 2020. *Burning Down the House: Newt Gingrich, the Fall of a Speaker, and the Rise of the New Republican Party.* New York. Penguin Press.

Index

About the Authors

Gary Lee Malecha, PhD, is the Tyson Distinguished Professor, Department of Political Science and Global Affairs, and interim dean of the Pamplin School of Business at the University of Portland (UP). Dr. Malecha joined the University of Portland faculty in 1992. He regularly teaches courses on Congress, the U.S. presidency, administration and public policy, American political thought, and food politics and policy in the United States and Europe. He has also offered courses in Western political thought and the politics of Central Europe and has taught in UP's study-abroad programs in the United Kingdom (London), Austria (Salzburg), and Central Europe (Salzburg, Vienna, Prague, and Krakow). Dr. Malecha's publications and research interests center on presidential leadership, congressional politics, presidential-congressional relations, institutional change, American political development and political thought, and contemporary issues in agricultural and food policy. He is the coauthor of *The Public Congress: Congressional Deliberation in a New Media Age*, published in 2012. Dr. Malecha is currently the faculty athletic representative at the University of Portland and in 2017–2018 served as the University of Portland's interim dean of the College of Arts and Sciences.

Daniel J. Reagan, PhD, is a professor of political science and the chair of the Department of Philosophy and Religious Studies at Ball State University, in Muncie, Indiana. Dr. Reagan joined the Department of Political Science at Ball State in 1989 and served as its Chair from 2014 to 2018. His primary area of expertise is American politics, and he has taught classes on a variety of topics, including public policy, the presidency, American national defense, the politics of health care, and Congress and the media. His publications address presidential leadership, career patterns in the House of Representatives, Senate confirmation hearings of Supreme Court nominees, deliberative democracy, and the impact of institutional rules on legislative behavior. He is the coauthor of *The Public Congress: Congressional Deliberation in a New Media Age*, published in 2012. He has served the state of Indiana in a number of capacities. He was appointed by Governor Frank O'Bannon to three state bodies: the Indiana Commission for Higher Education, 1998–2000, the Community College Policy Committee, 1999–2004, and the Indiana Education Roundtable, 2001–2003. The Indiana Commission for Higher Education appointed him to two positions: chair of the Statewide Transfer and Articulation Committee, 2000–2003, and program director of the Statewide Internship Initiative, 2002–2003.